MANAGEMENT INFORMATION SYSTEM

MANAGEMENT INFORMATION SYSTEM

A Conceptual Foundation

By

Ziauddin Khairoowala

Associate Professor
Department of Management and
Public Administration
Addis Ababa University
Ethiopia (Africa)

ANMOL PUBLICATIONS PVT. LTD.

NEW DELHI - 110 002 (INDIA)

ANMOL PUBLICATIONS PVT. LTD.
4374/4B, Ansari Road, Daryaganj
New Delhi - 110 002
Ph.: 23261597, 23278000
Visit us at: www.anmolpublications.com

Management Information System: A Conceptual Foundation

First Published, 2003

ISBN 81-261-1611-0

PRINTED IN INDIA

Published by J.L. Kumar for Anmol Publications Pvt. Ltd., New Delhi - 110 002 and Printed at Mehra Offset Press, Delhi.

Dedicated

to Our

PARENTS

Contents

Acknowledgements

The present work is an humble attempt to study the concept of Management Information System and its role in planning, controlling and operating different function of and organization by furnishing required information in the proper time frame to assist the decision-making process.

We are grateful to Mr. Naseem Ahmed Vice-Chancellor, A.M.U., Aligarh, for their moral support in completing this work.

We sincerely express my deep sense of gratitude to Professor Mushtaq Ahmed Khan, Deen and Chairman, Department of Commerce, A.M.U., Aligarh, who has been a constant source of inspiration and encouragement to us during the course of this study.

We are thankful to Professor Samiuddin and Prof. Nafees Beg, Ex-Deen & Chairman, Prof. Mehfoozur Rahman, Dr. (Mrs.) Salma Mehfooz, Professor Azhar Kazmi, Prof. A. Farooq Khan, Prof. M. Asif Ali Khan, Prof. Qamaruddin Khan, Prof. Sharifur Rahman, Prof. Badar Alam Iqbal, Prof. Mohd. Ali, Dr. Naimuddin Siddiqui, Dr. Ali Safdar Husain, Dr. Ziaul Ghani, Dr. Q.I.A. Bilgrami, Dr. Javed Alam Khan, Dr. Sibghatullah Farooqi, Dr. S.M. Imamul Haque, Dr. S. Husain Ashraf, Dr. A.Q. Khan, Dr. M. Talha, Dr. Imran Siddiqui, Dr. M. Mohsin Khan, Dr. Imran Saleem, Dr. Nawab Ali, Dr. Nasir Zameer Qureshi, Mrs. Sheeba Hamid, Dr. Mohd. Shamim, Dr. M. Ashraf Ali, Dr. Nafees A. Khan, Dr.

Mohd. Asir Khan, Dr. Mohd. Yameen, for their moral and academic encouragement in completing this work.

We are grateful to Prof. D. Amarchand, Madras; Syed Badre Alam, Madras; Prof. G.C. Agarwal, Allahabad; Prof. M.N. Ansari, Banaras; Prof. Nisar Ahmad, J.M.I., New Delhi; Dr. Noor A Khan and Dr. A.A. Ansari, J.M.I., New Delhi; Dr. Ziaul Islam, Madras; Dr. A. Jaffarulla; Dr. L. Ashraf Ali Khan for the encouragement to us during the course of writing this book.

In writing this book we have drawn upon the authorities on this subject and have acknowledged them at their proper places. Any lapses in acknowledgement are not deliberate and are likely to be due to oversight.

We are high indebted to our friends colleagues with whom I discussed the various problems from time to time and received their valuable suggestions. We would like to specially thank to Dr. Nasir Naeem, Dr. Mansoor Qutasha, Mr. Rahat Ali, Mr. Issam Taha, Ms. Chariyda Chantrungsri (Research Scholar).

We would like to thank Mr. Pradeep Sharma for typing the manuscript so neatly and efficiently.

We are thankful to M/s. Anmol Publications Pvt. Ltd. and its staff in bringing out this volume within a very short period of time so perfectly in a good shape.

Last but not least I would like to mention about the tremendous fore-bearance shown by my family members Mr. Hanif Uddin Khairoowala, Mrs. Shamim Hanif, Mrs. Rani Firdaus, Mohiuddin Khairoowala, Miss Naghma Zia and Miss Bushra Zia during the years of study which enabled me to complete this book.

1

Introduction

Management information system plays a vital role in the management of organization and decision-making. All the organizations have an information system composed of a variety of logical and physical resources. These resources are arranged or structured in an infinite number of ways. Moreover, because organization and information systems and dynamic resources, a structure one construct one day may not necessarily reflect the actual arrangement of these resources the next day.[1] Management information system in every organization is either manual or combination of man and machine underlying the management functions of planning, organizing, directing and controlling.

Management information system provide the managers with the accurate and timely informations that are relevant to his decision-making needs in regard to the establishment of objectives, policies and strategies of the organization. Managers obtain valuable insight into the system operations and the significant parameters related to the planning and control of operations while formulating their information requirements.[2]

Information requirements are never static. It exists in a world of concrete places and things, natural resources, and living persons. The sum of all these factors and forces is called the organizations environment. In fact, environment is a suprasystem of which organizations are sub-systems, each having identifiable boundaries that separate a business organization from its environments which is external and beyond the control of the organization. A business organization receives inputs from the environment, transforms them, and returns outputs.[3]

Business environment may be classified in various ways, such as local, national and international, or past, present and future, or economic and non-economic. The determinants of economic environment are fiscal policy, monetary policy, industry policy, physical controls of prices, income etc. The non-economic environment which comprises of socio-cultural, educational, legal, political, physical, historical and technological factors that has direct impact on business organizations.

Characteristics of Management Information System

Management information system was always been a key resource for any enterprise.[4] It is a combination of people, machines and procedures organized to provide past, present and future information relating to internal operations and external intelligence. It supports the planning, control and operations function of an organization by furnishing uniform information in the proper time-frame to assist the decision-making process.

Thus, a well designed management information system is likely to have the following characteristcs:

1. It is an integrated arrangement of furnishing required information at the right time and in a right form to the management. Integration management refers to study a complete view at the interlocking sub-systems that operate within a firm. Any new enterprise can start an MIS by attacking a specific subsystem, but unless its place in the total system is realized and properly reflected, serious shortcomings often crop up. Thus, an information system that blends information from several operational areas is a necessary element of MIS. MIS also requires perfect management because it is a costly and difficult to undertake.

2. It is a system consist of network of component parts and provide a flow of information to support decision- making process. By networking, the user of a personal computer can talk to other personal computers, turn the computer into a terminal and gain access to an organization's mainframe system, share the use of expensive printers, and tap into outside data cases. Networks are reshaping the manager's job. Electronic mail is lessening the manager's dependence on the telephone and traditional mail delivery service. Electronic messages can be communicated in seconds and if the receiver isn't at the terminal, there's no need for the sender to call back. Teleconferencing is reducing the need for travel. Group meeting can now take place among people thousands of miles apart. Tele-communicating permits some employees, including managers, to do their jobs at home and connect to the workplace by means a personal computer.[5] (See Fig. 1).

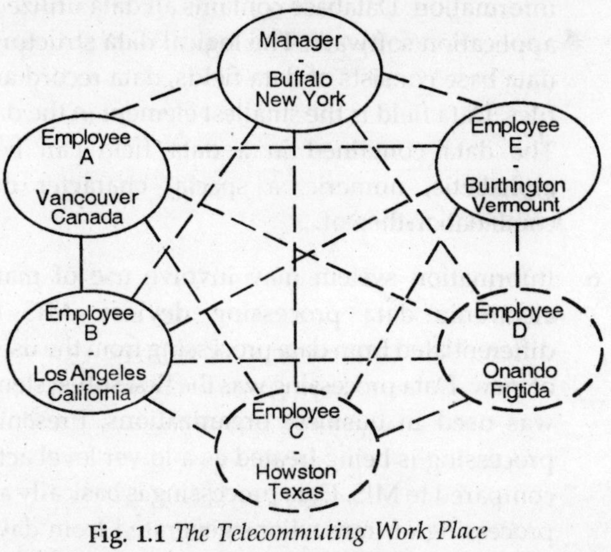

Fig. 1.1 *The Telecommuting Work Place*

3. Management information system is required at all

management levels. For top managers, the MIS provide information for strategic planning and management control. For strategic planning, the external sources of information—on economic conditions, technological development, the actions of competitors-assume paramount importance.[6]

4. For middle-level managers, such as division heads, are concerned with the current and future performance of their units. They therefore need information on important matters that will affect those units, large scale problems with suppliers, abrupt sales declines, or increased consumer demand for a particular product line. Thus, the type of information middle-level managers require consists of aggregate data from within the organization as well as from sources outside the organization.

5. Information system associated with establishment of database at a center unit that captures data close to its origin and converts this input into management information. Database contains all data utilized by the application software. The logical data structure of the data base consists of data fields, data record and data files. Data field is the smallest element in the database. The data contained in a data field can be either alphabetic, numeric, a special character or some combination thereof.

6. Information system may involve use of manual or electronic data processing devices. MIS can be differentiated from data processing from the users point of view. Data processing was the first sub-system which was used in business organizations. Presently data processing is being treated as a lower level activity as compared to MIS. Data processing is basically aimed at processing of transactions generated from day to day operations within an organization whereas MIS aims at

supplying information from the processed data to various levels of management to support their decision-making process. The use of computer for processing of data actually started with the data processing. The concept of MIS has evalued only recently within the organizations.

7. The role of MIS is basically that of generating and packaging of information in the useful quantums of knowledge. Moreover, MIS is a concept and an orientation toward which an information system design moves rather than being an absolute state.[7]

8. Computer provide MIS with such capabilities which are not possible in the manual information system. It may also involve use of manual devices. Often MIS is said to be associated with the use of computer. The computer helps in speed, accuracy, consistency in processing of data; handling large and wide variety of information, reduction of demand on clerical grade.

9. The system is composed of a collection of sub-system with varying degrees of integration among the parts. The system is generally viewed as a single entity. But is needs to be broken down into viable sub-systems which can be implemented one at a time. For this, a planning phase needs to be developed. Breaking down of MIS into meaningful sub-systems sets the stage for the planning phase. Many a time sub-systems can further be broken down into additional sub-systems. For example, every company in any society has three sub-systems: Financial, Administration control, Strategic planning, and Market Research. Each of these items work as a system and is therefore broken down into further sub-systems. For instance, strategic planning is broken down into production scheduling, control order processing and material control. On the same lines, material control is

down into factory and vendor sub-systems. Factory is broken down into Raw-material, work-in-progress, and finished goods. This is sub-system analysis is a must for laying boundaries to the problem, and thus making it possible for the designer to focus on manageable entities that can be assigned and computerized by selected systems and programming teams.

MIS makes a use of information communicating devices. The information communication is horizontal and vertical, throughout the requisition. It is necessary therefore, to employ in use sophisticated communication decision devices.

Role of Computer in MIS

Computer's role in MIS, is to be appraised on the following counts: forecasting, planning, control, modelling, systems analysis and facilities offered by the data base, as below:[8]

1. Forecasting

(a) Computer can perform such historical analysis as below speedly which may be difficult or even impossible manually.

(i) Data smoothing by means of moving averages or weighted, moving averages (including exponential smoothing) to disentangle the underlying from amidst irregularities.

(ii) Seasonal Analysis, Economic activity varies with reasons, viz. sales of ice cream. The seasonal analysis can be used to compute the seasonal indices.

(iii) Cyclical Analysis. Cycle of booms and depression can be descerned factoring an economic time series into trend, seasonal, cyclical and error components.

(iv) Correlation and regression analysis. Such relationship at the variance of sales is proportional to the mean sales etc. can be discovered. Multiple regression analysis involves a great deal of calculation and computer would be particularly useful here.

(v) Auto-correlation Analysis. There are some variable that have a time delay relationship, viz. sales of repair parts in a period is a function of the sales in the preceding period. Such relationships can be established.

(vi) Data Description. Various frequently distributions can be tried for a fit in the given data. Later, the goodness of the fit tests can be performed. Such summary statistics as mean, mode, median, SD, MAD, skewness etc. can be computed to describe the given data.

(vii) Optimal parameters of the selected forecasting model can be derived: for example, in simple exponential smoothing model what value of the smoothing coefficient to use? Different values are tried on the historical data and the one that yields the least comulative-squared error is selected for implementation.

(b) For routine forecasting too, computer provides considerable assistance. For example depend forecasts. For thousands of inventory items may have to be prepared every week, months, etc. which would be impossible manually but quite within the reach of the computer. Besides, such sophistications as adoptive response and tracking signals can be incorportaed to monitor the forecasts.

2. Planning

(a) Planning can be done more frequently and even

continuously. Because of constraints of computational and data processing abilities in manual systems, it used to be the practice to set reorder level annually. Important demand fluctuations were thus ignored resulting in higher stocks and proper service than is possible now in computerised systems where reorder levels can be revised much more frequently. Eilon reports 40% savings in stock-holding for the same service by periodically revising reorder levels on the basis of his extensive simulation experimentation.

(b) Sophisticated models for planning can be employed. For example, linear programming etc. can be used for production planning. In particular, project planning and control can be excellently carried out by means of CPM/PERT on the computer.

(c) Simulation can speed up evaluation of alternative plans. Simulation is a method reproducing the major element of a dynamic situation within the foreshortened time available through programming a computer. Thus, instead of waiting for 2 years to see the results of a capital investment project, the 2 year's experience may be simulated on the computer.

(d) The user interact with the computer to do better planning. For example, he may pose a question as what happens if the avertising budget is slashed by 15%. The computer, according to the mathematical model embedded in its program, would provide him with the consequences with which the user may not be satisfied. Based on the answer, however, he may structure another question and so on until the man and machine have iterated down to a satisfactory solution with a fine blend of their capabilities. The planner, together with this type of interactive computer can probe for data items, compare data, analyse relationships, test for various conditions evaluate, executive, and produce answers to many 'what if' questions. The interactive computer thus amplifies human intellect.

(e) For complex planning situations heuristic rules can be derived. Such a rule in production scheduling might be to schedule late items first, etc.

3. Control

(a) More comprehensive, varied, accurate and frequent reports can be produced where necessary.

(b) Statistical quality control techniques can be used to monitor marketing and financial ratios.

(c) Variance analysis plus other analyses which might assist in understanding both the reasons for variances and also the courses of action that will be corrective can be undertaken.

4. Modelling

Modelling can be tested for robustness simply or in conglomeration against historical or hypothesised data by simulation or otherwise. Sensitivity analysis can be performed to see to what extent the input variable affect the output variables. Computers can also assist in model building to sort out relationships.

5. Systems Analysis

Several alternative MIS designs can be evaluated by means of simulation experimentation.

6. Data Base Facility

Data is no longer vivisected departmentwise. All planner forecaster, supervisor, system analyst and modeller, can discharge their functions much better.

REFERENCES

1. John, G.B., Felix, R.S. and Gary, G., *Information System: Theory and Practice*, 3rd edition, John Wiley & Son, New York, 1983, p. 12.

2. Nauhria, R.N. and R. Prakash, *Management of Systems*, Wheeler Publishing, New Delhi, First Edition, 1995, p. 739.

3. Shukla, M.C., *Business Organization and Management*, S. Chand & Co. Ltd., New Delhi, 18 Edition, 1993, p. 16.

4. Amitabh Shah, "Information Management is Here", *The Times of India*, New Delhi, Sept. 18, 1996, p. 26.

5. Robbins, S.P., *Management: Concepts and Applications*, Prentice Hall, Englewood Cliffs, New Jersey, Second Edition, 1987, p. 506.

6. Charles, R. Litecky, "Corporate Strategy and MIS Planning", *Journal of Systems Management*, 32 No. 1 (January 1981), pp. 36-39.

7. Gordon, B. Davis, *MIS: Conceptual Foundations, Structure, and Development*, McGraw Hill Koogakusha Ltd., New Delhi, 1974, p. 7.

8. Verma, M.M. and R.K. Agarwal, *Management Information System*, King Books Education Publishers, New Delhi, 1998, pp. 58-61.

2

Management: Concept and Functions

Management has been defined in a variety of ways, but for our purpose it comprises the processes or activities that described what managers do in the operation of their organization. They plan, organize, initiate and control operations. They plan by setting strategies and goals and selecting the best course of action to achieve the plan. They organize the tasks necessary for the operational plan, set these tasks into homogeneous groups and assign authority delegation. They control the performance of the work by setting performance standards and avoiding deviation from standard.

Ralph C. Davis (1951)[1] defined Management as "Management is the function of executive leadership anywhere". Likewise, E.F.L. Breach (1953)[2] described the meaning of management as "the generic name for the total process of executive control in industry or commerce" being "the responsibility for the effective planning and regulation of the operations of an enterprise."

According to Peter Drucker (1954): "Management is a multi-purpose organ that manages a business and manages managers and manages worker and work."[3] But John F. Mee (1963) has defined the "management in different words a it is an art of securing maximum results with a minimum of effort so as to secure maximum prosperity and happiness for both employer and employee and give the public and best possible service."[4] William Spriegal (1942) says that "top management people are more concerned with administration while lower management people is in no way concerned with the administration of staff."[5] F.J. Wright rightly say that "Management comprises those functions which are involved in the carrying out of the decisions of the administration the former executes and implements the decision of the latter."

Dr. William R. Spriegal described as "Management is the managerial function, in carrying out the policies of administration, expands as the lower levels of supervision are reached while the administration function decreases in importance."[6] The same case of management was advocated by a British authority, Oliver Sheldon, he said that "Management proper is the function in industry concerned in the execution of policy, within the limits set up by the administration and the employment of the organization for the particular object set before it."[7] Similarly, G.E. Milward stated that "Management is the process and the agency through which the execution of policy is planned and supervised."[8]

Robert Presthus is of the view that "Management is the process by which individual and group effort is coordinated towards group goals."[9] The same view has been endorsed by J.H. Donnelly and others (1977) as "The process by which individuals and groups efforts is coordinated towards group goals."[10]

Koontz and Weebrich (1990) again defined management as "Management is the process of designing and maintaining an environment in which individuals, working together in groups, efficiently accomplish selected aims." This basic definition needs to be expanded:[11]

1. As managers, people carry out the managerial functions of planning, organization staffing, leading and controlling.
2. Management applies to any kind of organization.

3. It applies to managers at all organizational levels.
4. The aim of all managers is the same—to create a surplus.
5. Managing is concerned with productivity; this implies effectiveness and effluency/efficiency.

According to Mary Niles (1958): "Management is the function of an enterprise which concerns itself with the direction and control of the various activities to attain the business objectives. Management is essentially an executive function it deals particularly with the active direction of the human effort". Simultaneously George R. Terry (1968) advocated this view as "Management is a distinct process consisting of planning, organizing actuating and controlling, performed to determine and accomplish the objectives by the use of people and resources."[12] Likewise Dalton E. McFarland (1974) has depicted that "Management as that process by which managers create, direct, maintain and operate purposive organizations through systematic, coordinated cooperative human effort."[13]

Michale and others (1985) have depicted "Management as the process of planning, organizing leading and controlling the efforts of organization members and using all other organizational resources to achieve stated organizational goals."[14]

In the words of Stephen P. Robbins (1988): "Management refers to the process of getting activities completed efficiently with and through other people." The process represents the functions of primary activities engaged in by managers. The functions are typically labelled planning, organizing, leading and controlling. "Management is therefore concerned with not only getting activities completed (effectiveness), but also with doing so as efficiently as possible."[15]

J.L. Lundy (1992) has given the following definition of management which is as "Management is principally a task of planning, coordinating, motivating and controlling the efforts of others towards the specific objective."[16]

In other words, he says that "Management as a matter of principles is planning, coordinating, motivating and controlling, management aims at planning and controlling the activities of individuals and groups of individuals, directed towards the attainment specific objectives. It is also concerned with the coordination of the activities or efforts. Thus, management techniques are useful not only in business, but also in other fields."[17]

In a broad sense to E.F.L. Brech (1994) depicted Management as "a social process entailing responsibility for the effective (or efficient) planning and regulation of the operations of an enterprise, such responsibility involving: (a) the installation and maintenance of proper procedures to ensure adherence to plans; and (b) the guidance, integration and supervision of the personnel comprising the enterprise and carrying out its operation."[18]

According to G.R. Terry (1966): "Management is a distinct process consisting of activities of planning, organizing, actuating and controlling, performed to determine and accomplish stated objectives with the use of human beings and other resources."[19] This definition of management shows that there are six functions of management as they are often called, planning, organizing, actuating and controlling to achieve stated objectives.

Henri Fayol,the father of modern management, defines management as "to forecast and plan, to organize to command, to coordinate and to control."[20] The functions of organizations in order to achieve they stated objectives.

J.A. Stoner (1996) says that "Management is the process of planning, organizing, leading, and controlling the work of organization members and of using all available organizational resources to reach stated organizational goals." "Management is the practice of consciously and continually staping organization. All organization have people who are responsible for helping them achieve their goals. These people are called managers. These managers coaches, conductors, sales executives. May be more obvious in some organization than in others, but without effective management, organization are likely to founder."[21]

Stanley Vance (1956) says that "Management is simply a process of decision-making and control over the action of human beings for the express purpose of attaining predetermined goals."[22]

Lawrence A. Appley (1956) tries to simplify the meaning by describing the managers job as a "Human relations job that functions through several major activities" and that "human relation is the beginning and end of the management job."[23]

Lawrence A. Apple (1956)'s words of "Management is the development of people and not the direction of things. Thus, management is personnel administration."[24] According to Louis Allen (1958) "Management is what a manager does."[25]

The American Association says that: "Management is guiding human and physical resources into dynamic organization units which attain their objectives to the satisfaction of those saved and served and with a high degree of moral sense of attainment on the part of those rendering services."[26] W. Jack Duncan (1975) describes that "Management consists of all organizational activities that involve goal formation and accomplishment, performance appraisal, and the development of an operating philosophy that ensures the organization's survival within the social system."[27]

Harold Koontz and Cyril O'Donnell (1972) have depicted management as "Management is creation and maintenance of an internal environment in an enterprise where individuals, working together in groups, can perform efficiency and effectively towards the attainment of group goals, it is the art of getting the work done through and with people informally organized groups."[28] According to this definition managing is an art of creating favourable performance environment enabling the group of attain stated objectives and management is the body of organized knowledge, i.e. science which underlies the art. The definition clearly indicates that effective management is always contingency or situational, management. Creating of favourable managerial environment for joint efforts of people working in an organization for joint efforts of people working in an organization in order to accomplish planned objectives demands intelligent application of management knowledge to numerous and varied practical problems so that we can have the best results under the given situation or realities.

Kimball and Kimball are of the opinion, "Management is the process of decision making with an aim to exercise control over the activities of people involved in the business process."[29] Further, they said that "Management embraces all duties and functions that pertain to the initiation of the enterprises, it is financing, the establishment of all major policies, the provision of all necessary equipment, the outlining of the general form of organization under which the enterprise is to operate and the selection of the principles officers. The principal official primarily responsible to the controlling board is referred to as General Manager."[30]

Sir Charles Reynold says that "Management is the process of getting things done through the agency of a community. The functions of management are the handling of a community with a view of fulfilling the purposes for which it exists."

Elmore Peterson and E.G. Plowman says that "Management is a technique by means of which the purposes and objectives of a particular human group are determined, clarified and effectuated." According to James D. Mooncy and Alan C. Ruley

"Management is the art of directing and inspiring people." Lawrence A. Appley says, "Management is the art of getting things done through the efforts of other people." It concerns itself with guiding "human and physical resources into a dynamic, hard-hitting organize unit that attains its objectives to the satisfaction of those served, and with a high degree of moral and sense of attainment of the part of those rendering the service."

MEANING OF MANAGEMENT

Management is what managers does:

1. Planning
2. Organization
3. Directing
4. Coordiantion
5. Control

Essence of Management

Coordination of Human & Physical resources

Art of working with and through the people

Art and Science of Decision making and Leadership

Features of Management

The features of management are as follows:[31]

1. Management deals with multi-disciplinary discipline such as social science like Sociology, Psychology, Anthropology, Political Science, Quantitative Sciences, Mathematics, Statistics etc.

2. Management is applicable to all forms of human organisation whether it is profit-making or non-profit-making.

3. Management helps a manager to have a mental preparedness before he enters into any organisational work. It means any work should start with a plan and

shall end with control. The primary task of every manager is to get the best out of everybody through careful planning, proper direction and effective control. Rational optimum utilisation of the available resources to maximise the profit is the economic function of a manager.

4. A successful action is the outcome of attention and efforts taken by the managers. Successsful managers have an urge for accomplishment that people know should be done and they want to be done, but they realise probably can't be done if management is absent.

5. Management deals with the achievement of something specific expressed as an objective.

6. Management is an art of getting things done through people.

7. Management is an outstanding means for exerting real impact upon human life and passively viewed as inevitable. A manager can make progress, can bring hope, and can help and the better things in life can be achieved by the members of the group.

8. Management is Intangible. The presence of management is evidenced by the result of its efforts—orderliness informed employees, buoyant spirit and adequate work output.

9. Management is partly science and partly art.

10. Management is a profession. Profession involves the application of expert knowledge for solution of specific problems guided and governed by a code of conduct and social responsibilities.

11. Universal Application. Management is universal in character. The principles are working guidelines which are flexible and capable for adaptation to every

organisation where the efforts of human beings are to be coordinated.[32]

12. Management is necessary to all organizations. Not only the business organisations but non-business organisations like educational, religious, charitable and other social organisations also need management. Management is found everywhere as the distinct, separate and dominant activity. It is the prime institution in an organisation and its role cannot be undermined.[33]

Functions of Management

Management functions are closely inter-linked and interwoven in character. It may, however, be taken note of that there cannot be water-tight compartment for each of the functions of management. Each one is so interwoven that sometimes it becomes difficult to create a distinction between the levels and spheres of activity the different executives are required to perform. It is the organisational set up which helps such a distinction if the enterprise is scientifically organised with such of foresightedness and effective planning.

The various functions of management are as follows:[34]

Planning

Planning involves a rational and orderly thinking of ways and means with the help of which goals are desired to be achieved. It derives help from past events and anticipates action for the future. It is a thinking involving decision for future course of action depending upon the aim, the aim which is sought to be achieved through such a decision. It avoids rashness in approach consequently failure of action. To know what the work is, when, where and how the work is to be done and ultimately what is to be achieved are a few of the questions which are answered by planning as an action. In the words of Satya

Saran Chatterjee (i) diagnosis of the problem, (ii) development of alternatives, (iii) evaluation of alternatives, and (iv) selection of the best course of action are four most important steps of planning which embodies in itself the decision-making process.

Organisation

Organisation is a tool for achieving the objectives in a planned manner. It is a mechanism for purposeful action for the implementation of the policies and programmes.[35]

The organisation, thus, involves divisions and sub-division of the whole enterprise into departments, sections, jobs, positions and assignment of work according to the knowledge, skill and interest of individuals. The organisation decides inter-relationship between different functions, jobs, departments and personnel of the enterprise.

Besides the organisation is also entrusted with the function of taking a decision on delegation of authority which is helpful in establishment of a good inter-relationship between personnel on the one hand and between jobs, functions and departments on the other.

Thus it is necessary that organisational set-up should thoroughly be thought of and faithfully designed. In any management process good organisation results into the following benefits: (i) intelligent staffing, (ii) efficient direction, (iii) timely communication, (iv) beneficial co-ordination, (v) effective control; (vi) purposeful control; and (vii) purposeful leadership.

Direction

A good direction helps in (i) seeking co-operation from all the sundry; (ii) maintaining good inter-personnel and group relationship, (iii) active participation of workers in seeing through all aspects of the activities of the enterprise, (iv) inspiring and motivating the individuals to do their best;

(v) providing job satisfaction; and above all; and (vi) creating team spirit.

Control

A good controlling system ensures the following advantages to the enterprise: (i) the completion of plans according to pre-determined schedule; (ii) the evaluation of performances of individuals, groups and departments; (iii) the timely action, if schedule is not being kept; (iv) the adoption of speedy and timely remedial measures if lapses are detected; and (v) the plugging of loopholes, if any.

Motivation

Motivation is an act of providing personnels and inspiration to get to their jobs with zeal and enthusiasm and perform efficiently the work assigned to them. Management has a responsibility to utilise the capacity of its task force to the maximum. This could only be possible with the help of motivated personnel, who, if satisfactorily and effectively motivated, would pull their respective weight in right direction and give their loyalty to the enterprise whole-heartedly. They would then carry out the activities is allocated to them with purposeful sincerity.[36]

Co-ordination

Co-ordination today is not regarded as merely a management function but it has now become the essence of any management process. To give each division, unit and individuals of an enterprise. To give each division, unit and individuals of an enterprise a commonness of purpose, it is necessary that all activities of the enterprise should pull together and present a picture of unified unit. Approach to each aspect of the problem should be integrated and well co-ordinated. All these need co-ordination of activities so that the entire fabric may remain intact and splinter in efforts, cross-purpose working, inter-personnel department-section unit conflict may be avoided.

In order to have a creative force an unified and composite effort is needed. Co-ordination paves a way for such an effort which, thus, forms the very essence of the management process.

The following advantages a good co-ordination ensures (i) The whole enterprise presents a picture of unified approach to the problems of the enterprise, (ii) Splintering efforts do not spoil the working atmosphere in the enterprise, (iii) Cross purpose working yields to better understanding and efficient working; (iv) Inter-personnel and departmental conflicts seldom raise their ugly heads; (v) Commonness of purpose is achieved.

Staffing

The staffing function of management pertains to recruitment, selection, training, development and appraisal of personnel. There is a controversy whether staffing is a function of every manager in the organisation. Since every manager is concerned with management of human resources, he must perform the staffing and appraisal of human resources. The personnel department is set up to provide the necessary help to managers in performing their staffing or personnel function efficiently.[37]

Some authors do not view staffing as a separate function of management. Some argue that that it is a part of organising since it involves manning the position created by organisation process. It is also viewed by some as a part of direction as staffing activities are closely related to leadership, communication and motivation. However, in this book, staffing has been taken as a distinct function in view of the need to employ right types of people and to rain and develop them for the well-being of the organisation.

REFERENCES

1. Davis, R.C., *The Fundamentals of Top Management*, Harper & Bros. New York, 1951, p. 6.

2. Brech, E.F.L., *Principles & Practices of Management*, Longmans, Green & Co., London, 1953, p. 6.

3. Drucker, P., *The Practice of Management*, Harper & Row, New York, 1954, p. 17.

4. Mee, J.F., *Management Thought in a Dynamic Economy*, New York University Press, New York, 1963.

5. Spriegal, W. & Pradesh, P.C., *Organization & Management* 2nd Edition, Nirali Prakashan, Bombay, 1992, pp. 8-9.

6. Spriegal, W.R., *Principles of Business Organization and Operator*, p. 48.

7. *Philosophy of Management*, p. 32.

8. Milward, G.E., *An Approach to Management*, p. 34.

9. Presthus, R., *The Organization Society*, New York: Alfred A. Knopt, Inc. 1962.

10. Donnelly, J.H., Gibson, J.L. & Ivancevich, J.M., *Fundamental of Management*, (Dallas: Bus Publication, Inc., 1977, p. 4.

11. Koontz, H. & Weibrich, H., *Essentials of Management*, McGraw Hill Publishing Co., U.S.A., 5th Edition, 1990, p. 4.

12. Torry, G.R., *Principles of Management*, Richard D. Irwin, Inc., Home Wood, Illinois, 1968, p. 4.

13. McFarland, D.E., *Management Principles and Practices*, New York, MacMillan, 1974, pp. 4-6.

14. Michale H. Mescon, Management *Individual and Organization Effective*, 2nd Edition, New York, Harper and Row, 1985.

15. Robbins, S.P., *Management*, Prentice Hall, Englewood Cliffs, New Jersey, 2nd Edition, 1988, pp. 6-7.

16. Lundy, J.L. & Pradesh, P.C., *Organization & Management*, Forward Book Depot., New Delhi, 1994, p. 8.

17. *Ibid.*, p. 8.

18. Verma, M.N. & Aggarwal, R.K., *Principles of Management*, Forward Book Depot., New Delhi, 1994, p. 8.

19. Terry, G.R. & Franklin, S.G., *Principles of Management*, 8th Edition, All India Traveller Book Seller, New Delhi, 1996, pp. 4-5.

20. Verma, M.N. & Aggarwal, R.K., *Principles of Management*, op. cit., p. 9.

21. Stoner, J.A., Freeman, R.E. & Gilbert, D.R., *Management*,

Prentice Hall of India Pvt. Ltd., New Delhi, 6th Edition, 1996, p. 7.

22. Vance, S. , *Industrial Administration*, McGraw Hill Book Co. Inc., New York (1956), p. 3.

23. Appley, L.A., *Management in Action*, American Management Association, New York, 1956, p. 19.

24. Pigors D. and Myers C.A., *Personnel Administration*, McGraw Hill Book Co. Inc., New York, 1956, p. 4.

25. Louis Allen, *Management & Organization*, 1st Edition, McGraw Hill International Book Co., New Delhi, 1958, pp. 3-4.

26. Verma, M.M., Aggarwal R.K., *Principles of Management*, Forward Book Depot, New Delhi, p. 4.

27. Duncan, W.J., *Essential of Management*, Dryden Press Hisndale, Illinois, U.S.A., Jan. 1975, p. 5.

28. Harold Koontz and Cyril O'Donnell, *Principles of Management*, 5th Edition, New York, McGraw Hill, 1972, p. 1.

29. Kimball & Kimball, quoted by Verma, M.M. & Aggarwal, R.K., *Principles of Management*, Forward Book Depot, New Delhi, p. 8.

30. *Ibid.*

31. Pardesh, P.C., *Organisation & Management*, Nirali Prakashan, Pune, 1992, pp. 13-15.

32. Chhabra, T.N., *Principles & Practice of Management*, Dhanpat Rai & Co., Fifth Edition, 1997, pp. 6-7.

33. Mittal, A.K. & Aggarwal, S.B., *Principles of Management*, Sanjeeva Prakash, Second Edition, Meerut Cantt., 1998, pp. 22-25.

34. Varma, M.M. & Aggarwal, R.K., *Principles of Management*, Forward Book Depot, New Delhi, 1994, pp. 9-12.

35. Shukla, M.C., *Business Organisation and Management*, S. Chand & Company, 18 Edition, New Delhi, 1993, pp. 336-337.

36. Harold Koontz and Heinz Weihrich, *Essential of Management*, McGraw Hill International Edition, Fifth Edition, New Delhi, 1990, p. 319.

37. Chhabra T.N., *Principles and Practice of Management*, Dhanpat Rai & Co., Fifth Edition, 1997, p. 16.

3

Information: A Conceptual Approach

Information is vital to effective management. It is essential to know what is happening, where and when and what are its effects on the organization.

The information I have, is not what I want. The Information I want, is not what I need. The information I need, I do not have.

In the vast jungle of information one has to churn and get the desired data and then to interpret it from the synthesized matter so that proper inferences may be drawn. Which ultimately keep the Management to take decisions. People gather information directly by observing and experiencing events but when organizations become larger and more complex it becomes impossible for management, particularly in the middle and higher levels, to observe or experience all operations. In some forms of decentralized organization, management virtually never see the actual events and have to rely almost entirely on information provided through formal and informal channels. Although much valuable information is passed *via* discussions, meeting and causal conversation, such methods generally neither give a complete picture nor provide information in the correct form for the intended use.

The concepts of information can be defined as processed

data assisting management to discharge its functions. It consists of classified and interpreted data that are being used for decision-making. This is the most valuable assets required by management in order to plan and control business operations effectively. Now-a-days information constitute one of the factors of production. It is the input for production system.

Moreover, information is an imprecise term as commonly used. It can refer to raw data, organized data, the capacity of communication channel, etc. However, the uses of information in information systems are several which are as information adds to a representation, corrects or confirms previous information, or it has surprise value, or it tells something the receiver did not know or could not predict. In a world of uncertainty, information reduces uncertainty. It changes the probabilities attached to expected outcomes in a decision situation and therefore has value in the decision process. Information is data that has been processed into a form that is meaningful to the recipient and is of real or perceived value in current or perspective actions or decision.[1]

The definition recognizes both the value of information in a specific decision and the value of information in motivation, model building and background building affecting future decision and action.

According to R.N. Anthony and J. Dearden[2] information is fact, datum, observation, perception or any other thing adds to knowledge. The number 1000 taken by itself is not information, it doesn't add to anyone's knowledge. The statement that 1000 students are enrolled in a certain school is information. Information is obtained either by direct observation or by communication. Most of the manager obtained information by communication which is to be distinguished from reality. Besides, the purpose of information is to reduce a decision maker's uncertainty about the "state of nature". That is, about what is the actual situation in the real world, and the value of additional information should exceed its cost.[3]

Changing Trend in Information

Vasant Desai[4] watched a number of developing trends in information:

1. The business environment is undergoing sweeping changes in everything from technology to deregulation due to the restructing of companies and industries.
2. The demand for real time information and electronic information has grown up and further it will drew at a faster rate because of the technological improvement as business people has realised the advantage of real-time information efforts.
3. The information and communication technology such as computers, telecommunication and video are becoming increasingly interwined.

Functioning of Information

The number of Information which are as:

1. Information is needed to keep managers informed about what is going on.
2. The information is required to flow in a systematic manner in exact quality and quantity, that is neither too much nor too little, and to the respective persons in the organisation who require it. Hence, emerges the importance of management information system.

The rapid development in information technology (IT) have brought a significant change in the attitude of all corporate personnel, especially the senior managers, towards the applications of IT in a corporation.[5]

Review of Earlier Studies on Information

According to Claude E. Shannon and Warren W. (1949)[6],

"The amount of information obtained when you say something to me corresponds to the amount of uncertainty I have previous to your speaking of what you were going to say. If I was certain of what you were going to say. I obtained no information from your saying it."

Howard S. Levin[7] (1953) has pointed out in his book entitled 'Office Work and Automation' that "Information is a knowledge derived from the organization and analysis of data used for achieving the objectives of the business."

Adrain M. McDonough and Gordon Pask[8] (1963) are of the view that "informaion is an evaluated data in a specific situation, when uncertainty about it is zero, no further, information about it can be received."

Sinkovic[9] (1973) has discussed the method in which a relevant amount of information can be transferred in the guided system and further stated that it largely depends upon the structure of information system.

Gordon B. Davis[10] (1974) provided a conceptual framework of MIS. He defined that "Information is a processed data which is meaningful to the recipient for the purpose of decisions". The decisions can range from single, repetative to long-range strategic ones. The terms "data" and "information" are often used interchangeably, but there is a distinction in that. Data is the raw material that is processed to provide information. Information is associated with decision-making, and for this reason information can be considered as at a higher and more active level than data.

Bengt[11] (1982) writes that a number of approaches to information modelling has been presented in the decade of 1980 and 90s in which most approaches assumed that the correctness of information design is decided from intuitive considerations. He has advised three correctness criteria of information and information design namely satisfiability, completeness and consistency.

Kendall K.E. and Kendall J.E.[12] (1984) have mentioned in their joint paper that "A structured approach to observation of the decision-making environment is the only faithful way of obtaining information which as unobtainable through interrogation and examination".

N. Vittal[13] (1988) has stated in his paper that information is the life-blood of a society. People have to communicate with each other. The very evolution of human language from the time of the hunting community took place because of the need for communication. It is communication which has been built, a sense of identity and ultimate in its evolved form resulted in culture.

Review of Literature in India on Information

Single M.L.[14] (1992) has studied the impact and effectiveness of information system in public sector enterprises which varies with the growth in the MIS function and found it as behaviour oriented and not technique oriented.

Gupta A.P.[15] (1996) is of the view that information system today is the most vital component of infrastructure and is regarded as the key to all the complex task operations undertaken by national level system. Besides, the significance of information system is realized in almost all countries of the world especially by their informed leaders, that information is crucial to the life and performance of citizens, economic enterprises and nations of the world.

Review of Literature Abroad on Information System

Lee Thayer,[16] (1968) in his book captioned as *Communication and Communication System in Organization* has discussed the information system. He has laid stress that information is the raw material for thinking, decision-making, problem-involving, and for all human activities concerning psychological behaviour.

Steiner[17] (1969) is of the view that information flows are as important to the life and health of a business as the flow of blood is to the life and health an individual. High performance information systems can do much to promulgate organizational success. Computer based information systems have become increasingly important to modern business.

Goldkuhi and Lyythinen[18] (1982) have identified a new approach to information systems theory in which information system is regarded as a social and linguistic entity. The approach is based on a theory of communicative action, which studies infornaion and communication from the point of view of social interaction. According to the researcher, social interaction is basically an informal process. But much of the daily interactions is due to the formal process brought about by the organization design and structure—the structure of reporting relationships which has been overlooked in the study.

John G.B. Feler R. S. and Gary G.[19] (1983) found in their study that all organizations have an information system. This information system is a formal entity composed of a variety of logical and physical resources. From organization to organization these resources are arranged or structured in an infinite number of ways. Moreover, because organization and information system are dynamic resources of structure. We construct one day but it may not necessarily reflect the actual arrangement of these resources the next day. Thus, we need a concept that logically portrays the structure of an information system, that reflects all its physical resources, it is appropriate for any size of information system in any type of organize ion, and remains relatively constant. He was of the opinion that the most important item and stages in installation of MIS was transfer of the problem of designing and realization of the management from the sheer technical aspect to the organizational one. Further, the role of information pattern of communication and most important,—the information content has not been highlighted.

Leveson, Wasserman and Berry M. (1983)[20] have studied in their paper "A Behavioural Approach to the specification of Information System" and identified a multistep formal method used for information system design and development which include information analysis, semantic specification, verification of the specification.

Lethinen and Lyytinen[21] (1986) have stated that the main issue in information systems development is to specify correctly and unambiguously what an information system should accomplish and they call this information system specification. This stresses on the communication purpose, the information system has within an organization.

Mensah K.E.[22] (1984) in his article has discussed various techniques for the dissection of information needs of a business organization and progressing an information system design to address their need, they illustrate a formal method for deciding on the configuration of the information subsystems. He described three main criteria as a guide in recognizing the subsystem in any enterprises namely separability, comprehensibility and flexibility.

Robert G.M. Joel and James R.C.[23] are of the opinion that information system and the management groups are similar to the nervous system and brain of the human being. If sensing or reporting is faculty, incomplete or cut at some major juncture, the entire organism will become disoriented.

Data *Versus* Information

Data must be distinguished from information and the distinction clear and important for our purposes. Data once facts and figures that not cumulatively being used in a decision process and usually take from the historical records that are recorded and filed without immediate intent to network for decision-making.

Information consists of data that the netneved have

processed. Otherwise used for information or in... purpose, argument, or as a basis for forecasting or decision-making. In other words, the information processing system processes data into information or more precisely, the information processing system processes data in unusable form into usable data that is information to the intended recipient. The relation of data to information is defined as that of raw material to finished product. The analogy of raw material to finished product illustrates the concept that information for one person may be raw data for another—just as the finished product from one manufacturing division may be the raw material for another division. For example, shipping orders are information for the shipping room staff, but they are raw data for the vice-President incharge of the inventory. Because of this relation between data and information, the two words are used somewhat interchangeably.[24]

Definition of Data

Data are unconfirm, unripe events in isolation which do not convey any meaning to the recipient: (1) Information have some form, structure and convey some meaning to the recipient. (2) Data refers to material that has not been evaluated for its work to a specified individual, in a particular situation. (3) Information refers to inferential intended material evaluated for particular problem, for a specified individual, as a specific time, and for achieving a definite goal. (4) Data are facts, discrete items which may lack the necessary integration or ordering. (5) Information is the organized data with necessary integration and ordering. (6) Data are raw material unanalyzed numbers and facts about events, such as the number of computer disk produced per week. (7) Data item in information system are formed for characters. These may be alphabetic, numeric or special symbols. (8) Data processing is organized into data structures, file structure and data bases. (9) The term data is used to represent values of parameters which are mainly facts and figures. (10) The data is obtained from historical records, operational special surveys, interpersonal interactions or subject judgement.

The real distinction can be understand from the following chart:

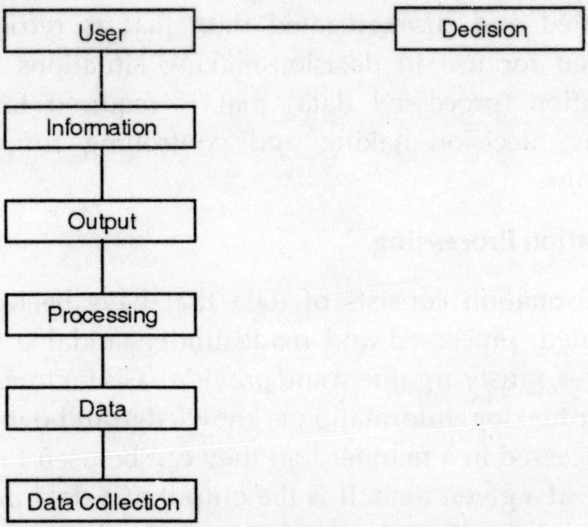

Data Processing

Data processing is the collection, transformation and retention of information. The organisation and its environment generate data which serves as input to data processing. We have the processing of internal and external data.

Data processing ultimately provides: (1) strategic information for strategic planning, (2) Tactical information for management (tactical) planning and control, (3) Operational (technical) information for operational planning and control, and (4) legal, conventional financial information required by the environment itself.

Definition of Information

Information has been defined as the cues or guidelines which have the potential to influence managerial decisions.

Manager is a decision-maker. Information is any fact or set of facts which is of value in specific decisions among alternative course of action. Information provides the means by which problems are recognized, defined, and eventually solved.

It can be concluded that information is an analysis of aggregated and disaggregated data that is retrieved and processed for use in decision-making situations. It is the information (processed data) that is required to perform planning, decision-making and controlling functions for operations.

Information Processing

Information consists of data that have been properly assimilated, processed and made understandable to derive inferences, satisfy argument and provide basis for forecasting or decision-making. Information is knowledge and data ordered and processed in a manner that they can be used for a given purpose at a given time. It is the output of a data processing system, such as a Profit & Loss (Income & Expenditure) Account and Balance Sheet of a banking company, which summarize information based on accounting data.

Producing Information from Data

An idea about how data are converted into meaningful information can be studied from the following discussions:[25]

1. The first and finest step in produce using information from data is correctly recording of data from an even or occurrence in some form such as sales slips, personnel forms, purchase order etc.

2. The second step is placing data elements into specified categories and predemand require specific category which provides meaning for the user. For example, sales data can be classified by inventory

type, size, customer, salesman, etc. and urgently file can be arranged by product code, usage value, classification of value etc.

3. The third step is arithmetic and logical manipulation of data i.e. computations to calculate employee's pay, customer's bill, student's grade point, etc.

4. The fourth step is placing data on to some storage media such as paper, microfilm, magnetic tape, magnetic disk etc. Where it can be kept for access and retrieval. It may be reproduced on to another magnetic disk or magnetic tape for further processing or security reasons.

Formal *Versus* Informal Information

The more formal information systems (via reports, operating statements, special analysis, variance returns, balance sheets etc.) have the advantages of comprehensiveness, consistency and reasonable accuracy but may suffer from the disadvantages of not meeting the exact requirements of the problem in hand, a lack of flexibility, time lag from even or operation to report and cost. In spite of these possible disadvantages the development of Management Informaion Systems (MIS) is vitally necessary in most organizations other than the very smallest. The distinction between formal and information is a third important concept.[26]

Examples of formal information include: legal requirements, government legislation, union contracts, accounting, procedures, planning requirement, organizational budgets, job demands communication requirements, control needs, stock-holders, creditors and demands, problem situations, and general decision-making processes. Pay cheques, invoices, purchase orders, and receiving tickets are all examples of structured forms of formal information. Status reports, variances probabilities, return on investment, reorder points, contribution margins, and traditional accounting statements are highly formalized forms of information.

Informal information includes opinions, judgments hunches, intuition, hearsay, personal experiences, "grapevenes", rules of thumb, gossip, assumptions, and so forth.

Evaluation of Information

The information which they receive on four factors viz. its quality, timeliness, quantity, and relevance to management needs to the evaluated.[27]

1. *Information on Quality*: The more accurate the information the higher its quality and managers can rely on it when making decisions.
2. *Information Timeliness*: The information provided by an information system must be available to the right person at the right time for the appropriate action to be taken.
3. *Information Quantity*: Managers can hardly make accurate and timely decisions without sufficient information. However, managers are often inundated with irrelevant and useless information.
4. *Information Relevance*: Similarly, the information that managers receive must have relevance to their responsibilities and tasks. The personnel manager does not need to know inventory levels—and the manager-in-charge of recordering inventory doe not need to know about the status of staff members in other departments.

Characteristics of Information

The characters of Information can be studied from the following discussions:

1. Quality of Information varies due to bias, or errors,

or from delay. If the bias of the information is known the appropriate adjustment can be make by the recipient, the problem is to detect the bias and then correction is relatively easy. Errors are a more serious problem because there is no simple adjustment. Errors may arise due to: (a) incorrect data measurement and collection; (b) failure to follow correct processing procedures; (c) loss or non-processing of data; (d) use of incorrect files; (e) mistakes in processing, and (f) deliberate falsification.

Error Correction

The difficulties with errors can be overcome by: (a) more internal controls (e.g. Batch totals, check digit verification, etc.) (b) careful testing of procedures and programmes prior to operational running, (c) internal and external auditing procedures, (d) recognition that in particular areas errors are likely to exist so that data should have condience limits added.

Timing: Information leads to action. Therefore it is important to consider the timing of the whole process from data collection through processing to the resulting action and not just a part of the sequence.

Faster is not necessarily better: Information which is produced more quickly perhaps by the addition of expensive on-line equipment, is not necessarily better information. The use of information is to improve the resulting decisions. If the increased speed results in improved decisions then it may be worthwhile. The one thing that can generally be said about speedler information is that it will be more expensive information. Nevertheless, speed of information production of often a critical factor and speedly prepared, reasonably accurate information may enable decisions to be taken which more than recompense any extra information processing costs. One of the major complaints made by managers about MIS is that information is often received too late to be used effectively.

Levels Handling Information

Typically information moves up several levels in the hierarchy before decisions are made. The decision is then communicated down through the various levels before action is taken. This movement through the organization level causes delay and may introduce errors into the system. For example, delay in implementing action, may cause negative feedback to become positive feedback. Repeated delays in obtaining decisions may cause unofficial *ad-hoc* information systems to develop to overcome the faults in the official system. In general, actions should be taken as low down a possible and the number of reporting levels kept to a minimum.

Presentation: This must be tailored to suit the recipient, the data and the actions expected. A project investment analyst may well require very detailed quantitative information in terms of probabilities and confidence limits but a factory charge hand may be much better served by a simple, graphical presentation. In general, visual information to show trends and standard has been shown to be more rapidly a similated. Long codes should be avoided as research seems to indicate that the number of symbols people can hold in short-term memory and process effectively is from 5 to 9 with a common limit of 7.

Relevance and Materiality: To be of maximum value information should be relevant for the decision in hand and insignificant or non-material matter should not be presented to the manager. This is a clear enough principle but its application is not always so straightforward. The problem is that the information supplied may be used for various decisions and what is irrelevant for one decision may highly relevant for another. This problem may be particularly acure where centralized information handling is carried out and decision-making is largely decentralized. There is no ready answer to this problem but it can be minimized by full management involvement in the design of the MIS experienced information specialists who are aware of managerial problems and continuing, close liaison between managers and information specialists. A responsive MIS with a short turn round time will also have more change of producing relevant information.

Volume and Detail: The capacity of people to accept information inputs and produce meaningful responses is limited. More information is available than people can cope with so therefore this introduce their own importance filters and screen out factors considered unnecessary to the situation. These personal filters increases in stress conditions until only the most important factors come through. For example, consider the difference in a foreman's information filters during normal production and an unexpected assembly line stoppage.

MIS and Volume: MIS designers who proudly claim that their system produce more management information have missed the point. Managers are already swamped by the quantity of information. What they require are systems which shift, summarize, codify, point out exceptions and trends, consolidate filter, highlight, carry out all the calculation involved in short do the donkey work for them and present then with the minimum amount necessary for them to be able to take effective actions. The production of information is merely a means to an end—which is effective decisions and actions.

Detail: Detail should not be confused with accuracy. Every superfluous character means extra storage, mere delay, extra processing, extra assimilation and possibility poorer decisions. The basic rule, as with volume is as little as possible consistent with effective decision-making. The level of detail should vary with the level of the hierarchy, the higher the level, of detail should vary with the greater degree of compession and summarization although the information will probably related to a boarder functional area. At lower level where the responsibility is much more localized, more detail is likely to be required.

Frequency and Regularity: Routine information equivalent of system inputs and outputs are produced at regular intervals, hourly, daily, weekly, monthly and so on. This is for two practical reasons, the necessary for monitoring the system and convenience of processing. Routine basic information should be distinguished from deviation information which also tends to be produced at similar regular intervals. For this type of information the appropriate frequency should be established after considering after that length of period is a deviation from standard, or trend towards such a deviation, likely to appear.

Value of Information: Information has no value in itself; its value derives from the value of the change in decision behaviour caused by the formation being available minus the cost of producing the information. There is a tendency to assume that more information, earlier or more upto data information, more accurate information etc., is all better information. It may be better information but only if it improve the resulting decisions, otherwise it has no value.

Cost of Information: The production of information only incurs costs which are often considerably. Benefits only arise from actions. When considering extensions to MIS or enhancements to computer systems, or the hiring of more staff to produce information, the comparison must be between the extra costs and the values arising from the hopefully improved actions. An incorrect approach, although very common, is to compare various ways of producing the same information and choosing the cheapest method without even relating it to the improved actions.

Enhancing the Value of Information: it will be recalled from the preceding chapter that investigations into practical information systems have found that much of the information produced is ignored by the managers concerned. It follows that information which is ignored cannot influence the decision-making process and therefore it has no value. To enhance the information it must be capable of being used and the investigations show that information which has the following characteristics is more likely to be used.

Relevance: i.e. appropriate to the manager's sphere of activity.

Timing: i.e. produced and available to the manager in time for him to use.

Accurate: i.e. sufficiently accurate for it to be relied upon the manager and for the purpose for which it is intended.

Understandable: i.e. in a form and format readily usuable by the manager.

Communication Theory

Having considered information and some of its characteristics it is necessary to consider how information is transmitted. The information system has input in the form of data received from internal and external sources. The process is in charge of transforming data into useful information. The output is the relevant information useful for planning, decision-making and controlling the enterprise activities. The controller is the decision-maker who uses the information.

The information system provides necesssary legal and traditional financial information as well as that which is demanded by managers at strategic, tactical and operational level of management.

To manage a business well is to manage its future. Management of future implies management of information-external as well as internal information. Today a mass of information is generated by internal as well as external sources. Since 1960, we are having an information explosion. Hence, management must have well-organized and upto-date MIS on the basis of which management at all levels can take prompt and sound decisions on all problems in any area of business. MIS is an integral part of decision-making process at all levels of management.

Functions of Information System

Functions of an information system can be broadly classified into two groups:[28]

(a) Data Collection

(b) Data Managaement

(a) *Data Collection*: Who should collect what data and what form and how often? The nature and the form of data will vary from organization to organization depending upon its objectives. The manner of data collection will depend upon the purpose for which data is collected. After collection of data irrelevanted data should be filtered out and the relevant data should be properly classified and tabulated so that it can be used easily when needed.

(b) *Data Management*: A good data management system must have the following characteristics:

(i) it should be efficient in respect of routine processing operations;

(ii) it should be flexible;

(iii) the retrieval of information in case of an enquiry should be efficiently accomplished.

Any data management system should be capable of giving efficient service in terms of day-to-day processing of information. At the same time, the system design should not be rigid. With the changes in conditions, demand on the information system may change. It may be that same information may be needed in different format or different levels of aggregation may be needed. An efficient system should be able to quickly respond to these types of demand on the system.

REFERENCES

1. Gordon, B.D. and Olson, M.H., *Management Information System*, McGraw International Edition, Second Edition, New Delhi, 1985, pp. 200-201.
2. Anthony, R.N. and Dearden, J., *Management Control System: Text and Cases*, D.B. Transporvales Son & Co. Pvt. Ltd., Second Edition, Bombay, 1981, pp. 94-95.
3. *Ibid.*, p. 95.
4. Vasant Desai, *Principles of Bank Management—Principles, Planning and Programming*, Himalaya Publishing House, First Edition, New Delhi, 1993, pp. 375-76.
5. *The Times of India*, "Information Management is Here", New Delhi, Sept. 18, Wednesday, 1996, p. 26.
6. Shannon, C.E. and Warren, W., *The Mathematical Theory of Communication*, Urbana : University of Illinois Press, 1949, p. 7.
7. Levin, H.S. , *Office Work and Automation*, John Wiley & Sons, New York, 1956, p. 122.
8. McDonough, A.M., *Information Economic & Management System*, McGraw Hill Book Co., New York, 1963, p. 71.
9. Sinkovic, V., "Optimization of Information System Structure", *Informatological Yogoslavia*, Vol. 5 (1/4), Yogoslavia, 1973, pp. 23-33.
10. Davis, B. Gordon, *MIS: Conceptual, Foundations, Structure and Development*, 1st Edition, International Student Edn., New Delhi, 1974, pp. 32-33.
11. Bengt Lundberg, *Correction of Information Models*, Sweden, 1982.
12. Kendall, K.E. and Kendall, J.E., *A Structured Approach to Observation of the Decision-Making Environment: Information and Management*, Vol. 7(1), Nebraska, 1984, p. 1.
13. Vittal, N., "Social Impact of Information Age: Democracy and

Government of Line", *Journal of Communication, Computers and Net Work*, New Delhi, Feb. 1998, pp. 46-48.

14. Singla, M.L., "MIS is Public Sector Undertaking a Perceptual Study", *Indian Management*, December, 1992, p. 14.

15. Gupta, A.P., "MIS at National Level in India, Analysis of Problems and Issues", *Viakalpa*, Vol. 21, July-Sept. 1996, pp. 3-14.

16. Lee Thayer, "Communication and Communication System in Organization", *Management and International Relations*, Home Wood III, Richard D. Irwin, 1968, pp. 18-19.

17. Steiner, G.A., *Top Management Planning*, Toronto Collier, MacMillan, 1969, p. 475.

18. Gron Goldkuhl and Kalle Lyytinen, A., *Language Action View of Information Systems*, Sweden, 1982.

19. John, G.B., Feler, R.S. and Gary, G., *Information System, Theory and Practice*, John Wiley & Sons. Third Edition, New York, 1983, p. 12.

20. Leveson, N.G., Wasserman A.I., and Berry, M., "Basis: A Behavioural Approach to the Specification of Information Systems". *Information Systems*, Vol. 8, No. 1, Great Britain, 1983, pp. 15-23.

21. Lethinen, E. and Lyytinen Kalhe, Action Based Model of Information System", *Information System*, Vol. III, No. 4, Great Britain, 1986, pp. 299-317.

22. Mensah, K.E., "Identifying Subsystems in Information System Analysis", *Information Systems*, Vol. (9), USA, 1984, p. 181.

23. Robert, G.M., Joel, F.R. and James, R.C., *Information System Modern Management*, III Edition, Prentice Hall of All India Pvt. Ltd., New Delhi, 1987, p. 67.

24. John, G.B., Felix, R.S. and Gary, G., *Information System: Theory and Practice*, John Wiley & Sons, Third Edition, New York, 1983.

25. Nauria, R.N. and Rajnish Prakash, *Management of System*, Wheeler Publishing, First Edition, New Delhi, 1995, pp. 732-33.

26. John, G.B., Felix, R.S. and Gary, G., *Information System: Theory and Practice*, John Wiley & Sons, Third Edition, New York, 1983.

27. Stoner, A.F. and Freeman, R.E., *Management*, Prentice Hall of India, Fifti Edition, New Delhi, 1992, pp. 666-667.

28. Chhabra, T.N., *Principles and Practice of Management*, Dhanpat Rai & Sons, 5th Edition, New Delhi, 1991, p. 578.

4

System and Sub-System

The term system has become quite popular in recent years. One speaks of an educational system, computer system, software system, solar system, and many others. The system those activities which were required for data processing. The development of the digital computer and its related technology popularized the use of the word systems.[1] The equipment which functions together to do computer processing are called computer system. Systems can be physical. A physical system is a set of elements which operate together to accomplish an objective or in other words a system is composed of interacting. Parts that 'operate together' to achieve some objective or purpose. A system has been variously defined as "an assemblage of things, forming a computer or unitary whole".[2]

In other words system may be defined as "A system is a set of interrelated component and objects with the relationships between the objects and their attributes."

"A system may be described generally as complex of elements or components directly or indirectly related in a causal network such that each component is related to least some others in a more or less stable way within any particular period of time".

"An assembledge of interrelated and interdependent elements forming a unified whole."

"A system is a set of interacting elements, interacting with each other to achieve a predetermined objective or goal".

"A system is set of element forming an activity or a processing procedure seeking common goal by operating on data or energy and matter in a time reference to yield information or energy and matter."

According to Carl Heyel[3]— "A system is a regular, orderly way of doing something or arrangement of interdependent activities and related procedure. All systems are parts of larger systems". A bank is system and it division, various departments, functions, units etc. are subsystem. Similarly, Banking Industry is a system and a Bank is sub-system.

Webster define 'system' as a set or arrangement of people, things and concepts, which are related to form a unity to achieve a mutual goal. A system is a regular, orderly way of doing something. For purpose of its use in MIS, the system module given below is a useful method of describing the related things that are brought together to form a unity. The name 'system' may be applied to describe a productive organization, such as an automobile factory, a cement manufacturing plant, or a textile manufacturing organization as well as service organizations such as Hospital, Bank, University, Departmental Store.

Robert G.M. and others[4] have defined 'system' a "set of element joined together for a common objective. A sub-system is part of a larger system with which we are concerned. All systems are parts of larger systems. For our purposes the organization is the system, and the parts (divisions, departments, functions, units, etc.) are the sub-systems."

According to R.C. Hopkins[5], "A system is a set of elements forming an activity or a processing procedure/ scheme seeking a common goal or goals by operating on data and matter in a time reference to yield information or matter."

Some specific cases illustrate the somewhat abstract definition:

1. *Manufacturing System:* A group of people, machines,, and facilities (a set of elements) work to produce a specified number and type of products (seek a common goal) by operating on product specifications, schedules, raw materials, sub-assemblies, and electrical power converted to mechanical power (operate on data, matter and energy) to yield the specified products and information by the data the customer wants them (to yield matter in a time reference).
2. *Management Information System*: A group of people, a set of manuals, and data processing equipment (a set of elements) select, store, process, and retrieve data (operate on data and matter) to reduce the uncertainty in decision-making (seek a common goal) by yielding information for managers at the time they can most efficiently use it (yield information in a time reference).
3. *Business Organization System*: A group of people (set of elements) gathers and processes material and informational resources (form an activity) toward a set of multiple common goals including an economic profit for the business (seek common goals) by performing financing, design, production, and marketing (operating on data, energy, energy and matter) to achieve finished products and their sale at a specified minimum rate per year (yield matter in a time reference).

Review of Literature on System and Sub-System

Stanley Vance[6] (1956) has expressed "the significance of MIS in the context of management that it helps in the process of decision-making and control over the action of human beings for the purpose of attaining predetermined goals."

Management Information

Estees, H.M.[7] (1966) has stated that "Management Information is growing by the microsecond and even nanosecond. One cannot turn of the flow, therefore, it is better to learn to control it". Likewise, information is the net value obtained from the process of matching the elements of a present problem with appropriate elements of data.

Management System

Ivancenrich and Donnelly[8] (1976) Management System (MS) may be defined as an "approach in its organization—decision-making in which the principles of scientific methods are utilized to find solution to management problems". The application of Management Science to MIS represents a tremendous advance over the disorganized collection of information and management by experience based on feelings. Management science requires managers to define their problems and assumptions carefully, usually in terms that may be quantified and measured, so that they may achieve better solutions.

System and Sub-system

Robert G.M.[9] (1987) in his famous book "Information System for Modern Management", examines the difference between system and sub-system as a set of elements forming an activity or a processing procedure/scheme seeking a common goal or goals by operating on data or energy and matter in a time reference to yield information, energy and matter. A sub-system is part of a larger system with which we are concerned. All systems are parts of larger systems. For our purposes, the organization is the system, and the parts (divisions, departments, functions, units, etc.) are the sub-systems. The system concept of MIS is therefore one of optimizing the output of the organization by connecting the operating sub-systems through the medium of information exchange.

Functions of System

The main functions of the system are as follows:[10]

1. Establishment of file with data elements is one of the functions of system.
2. The another classical function of the data processing system is the maintain of file.
3. The third infront out function of system is to generate reports tailored to management specification.
4. The final major function of a system is information retrieval.

Parts of the Organization System

The basic parts of the organization system are the individual, the formal organization, the informal organization, leadership styles, and the physical setting. These parts and their interdependencies can be described as:[11]

1. *The Individual*: The basic part of the system is the individual—his personality, motives, and attitudes. The concern here is not so much, what the individual can contribute to the organization but now he perceives the fulfillment of his goals from participation in it.
2. *The Formal Organization*: The structure of the formal organisation is composed of the assignment and interrelated pattern of tasks.
3. *The Informal Organization*: Informal organisations interacts with the formal organization as well as with the individual.

Classification of Systems

The classification of system is neither fixed nor rigid and it is possible to have one classification for particular purposes at one time and another classification at another time. The following commonly accepted classifications are the most important ones for a study of business and information systems.[12]

Conceptual System

Conceptual systems are concerned with theoretical structures, which may or may not have any counterpart in the real world.

Empirical Systems

Empirical systems are generally concern with operational systems made up of people, materials, machines, energy, and other physical things, although electrical, thermal, chemical, information and other such systems.

Natural System

Natural systems abound in nature. The entire ecology of life is a natural system and each organism is a unique natural system of its own. The water system of the world, at least before man affected it, was a natural system. Our own solar system is a natural system.

Man-made System

Man-made systems were formed when men first gathered in groups to live and hunt together. They now appear in infinite variety all about us and extend from the manufacturing system of a company to the system of space exploration. Their objectives likewise vary tremendously. One system may be concerned with national defence; another may be a transportation system. A business organization is a system with many smaller systems included—production, accounting, and so on—as well as others such as communication systems and office layout systems overlaid upon the main economic organization of people.

Social System

Social system is made up of people. Business

organizations, government agencies, political parties, social clubs, and technical societies are examples of systems that may be so studied.

Machine System

In the area of information system the machine elements such as computer and computer programmes are relatively closed and determinities.

Man/Machine System

Man/machine system can emphasize the machine and use the human only as monitor of machine operation on the other extremes it emphasis on human so that machine perform supporting role such as to provide computation and search of data.

Deterministic System

A deterministic system operates in a perfectly predictable manner. The interaction among the parts is known with certainty. For example, in electric motor an input of a particular voltage will produce an output of a known number of revolutions per minute. A computer program is another example of a deterministic system, that is, a given data input will produce a defined output.

Probabilistic or Stochastic Systems

The probabilistic system can be described in terms of probable behaviour but a certain degree of error is always attached to the production of what the system will do. An inventory system is an eagle of products system. The average stock, the average demand or the average replishment time may be predicted but the exact value of these factor at any given time is not known.[13]

Open System

An open system is one that interacts and exchange

information material or energy with its environment. The exchanges may include random and undefined inputs. All systems containing living organisms are obviously open systems because they are affected by what is sensed by the organisms. In a more important sense, organizations are usually systems operating within larger systems and are therefore, open systems. For example, a company's marketing organization is a system that is a part of the larger system, the entire company. The company in turn is a system within the larger industry system. Other examples of open system are biological systems (such as man) and organizational system open systems tend to have a quality of adaptation which means they can adopt to changes in their environment in such a way as to continue their existance.

The fact that a company interacts with its environment—larger system—makes that individual company an open system. The open system may be further identified by its individually small influence on its environment and inadequate feedback of information from the environment. As business managers will readily agree, they must somehow manage their companies in great ignorance about the future impact of environmental conditions. The environmental system with which they can best contend is the particular industry system of which they are apart. Continuing in this direction then, one note that the industry is part of the national economic system, which in turn is a system within our society. Our society is a system within the world system; the world system is a part of the solar system; and so on into the unknown.

Closed System

A closed sytem is defined in physical as a system which is itself contained. It does not exchange maternal information, or energy with environment. What environment surrounds the closed system does not change, or if it does, a barrier exists between the environment and the system to prevent the system from being affected. The scientists who devises a laboratory system to measure the elasticity of metal is assuming a closed system such that environmental changes that would affect his results are avoided. Problems in business are sometimes resolved as if a closed system existed in order to simplify the situation enough so that at least a first approximation can be obtained. System in manufacturing are, for example designed to minimize uncounted exchange with the environment outside the system. In other words the system designed to be as closed as possible. A computer programme is a relatively closed system because it accepts only primarily defined inputs, processes them, and provides previously defined out fruits. The closed system is that has only consulted and well defined inputs and outputs. It is not subject destructions from outside the system.[14]

Some authors distinguish further between open system that are simply influenced passively by the environment and those that react and adapt to the environment. These sub-classes are designated as nonadaptive and adaptive systems.

Systems Approach

A knowledge of systems concepts avoids taking a piecemeal approach to problems because of the awareness that there are interactions between parts of the systems, that the overall system characteristics are usually greater that the sum of the characteristics of the individual constituents, and that alterations cannot be made to some parts of a system without considering the effects on the system as a whole.

System Approach to MIS

Computerised MIS has become a normal feature of a computerized business in the development countries.

A system may be defined as a set of units and elements which are integrated to perform the objective. A corporation consists of divisions, departments, sections, functions, etc., which are joined together in carrying out a common goal. Systems approach centres attention upon objectives for which the organization has been established. It stresses the inter-dependence of elements so that manager is constantly forced to view the elements or parts of a business in relation to developing information processing system for management planning and control.[15]

The systems approach forces the manager to consider his business organization as a network of information, with flow of information, providing decision-makers at all levels with the relevant information in order to make all types of decisions.

These information communication systems intercorrect together all components needed to operate business successfully. The systems concept of MIS aims towards optimising the processing of information from various units and provide necessary basis for performing management functions from the systems view-point. For example, marketing must be integrated with research and development and production, similarly, production with finance, and so on. The MIS provides capability to exchange relevant information about the total organization to an operating element. This provides a high degree of synergism which enhances optimum decisions rather than suboptimum ones.

The systems approach has been described by Thome and Willard[16] thus:

The Systems Approach is an orderly way of appraising a human need of a complex nature, in a let's stand-back-and-look-at-this-situation-from-all-its-angles frame of mind, asking oneself.

How many distinguishable elements are there in this seeming problem?

What cause-effect relationships exist among these elements? What functions need to be performed in each case? What trade- offs may be required among resources once they are defined?

REFERENCES

1. John, G.B., Felix, R.S. and Gar, G., *Information System Theory & Practice*, Second Edition, John Wiley & Sons, New York, 1983, p. 9.

2. Churchman, C.W., *Prediction and Optional Decision*, Prentice Hall, 1961, p. 100.

3. Robert, G.M., Joel, F.R. and James, R.C., *Information System for Modern Management*, Prentice Hall of All India Private Ltd., Third Edition, New Delhi, 1987, pp. 4-7.

4. Hopkins, R.C., "A Systematic Procedure for System Development", *IRE Transactions, on Engineering Management*, June 1961, p. 85; and Davis, O. Ellis and Fred, J. Ludwig, "Systems Philosophy", (Englewood Cliffs, N.J., Prentice Hall Inc., 1962).

5. Vance, S., *Industrial Administration*, McGraw Hill Book Co., Inc., New York, 1956, p. 3.

6. Estees, H.M., "Will Managers be Overwhelmed by the Information Explosion", *Armed Forces Management*, Dec. 1966, p. 84.

7. Lyon Ivancenrich and Donnelly, *Management Science in Organizations*, Goodyear Publishing Co. Inc., Pacific Palisades, California, 1976, p. 6.

8. Robert, G.M., Joel, F.R. & James, R.C., *Information System for Modern Management*, Prentice Hall of All India Pvt. Ltd., IIIrd Edition, New Delhi, 1987, pp. 4-5.

9. D.R. Hampton, *Modern Management: Issues and Ideas*, Prentice Hall Pvt. Ltd., New Delhi, 1994, pp. 210-211.

10. Chris Argyris, *Personality and Organization*, New York: Harper & Row Publishers, 1957.

11. *Ibid.*, Chris Arguris, 1957.

12. Stanfrod, L. Optner, *Systems Analysis for Business and Industrial Problem Solving*, Englewood Cliffs, N.J., Prentice Hall Inc., 1965.

13. Garden, B. Davis, *Management Information System: Conceptual Foundations*, McGraw Hill Ltd., Tokyo, 1974, pp. 86-89.

14. *Ibid.*

15. Sherlekar, S.A. and Sherlekar, J.S., *Principles of Business Management*, Himalaya Publishing House, New Delhi, 1996, pp. 444-445.

16. G. Thom and R.G. Willard, "The System Approach: A Useful Concept of Planning", *Aerospace Management* (General Electric Company), Fall/Winter, 1966, p. 25.

5

Management Information System

Introduction

Management Information System (MIS) is an industry within industry. The accelerating complexities of modern organs are demands new dimensions in management system. Hence, in the age of system—the managers of today be skilled in the functional areas through as System Approach to Management coupled with the ability to participate in the design and utilization of computer based information system.

Characteristics Features of a Management Information System

According to Jorge M. Scott, MIS is a comprehensive and coordinated set of information subsystems which are rationally integrated and which transform data into information in a variety of ways to enhance productivity in conformity with the manager's style and characteristics on the basis of established quality criteria.

1. MIS is the combination of men, machine and procedures for collecting pertinent information from the internal and external source of a firm, and processing these informations for the purpose of facilitating the process of decision-making.

2. MIS is not new; only its computerization is new. Before computers, MIS techniques existed to supply managers

with the information that would permit them to plan and control operations.

3. The computer has added one or more dimensions such as speed, accuracy and increased volumes of data and permit the consideration of more alternatives in a decision.

4. One may define the term MIS as a system to provide management with needed information on a regular basis. In theory this system can be manual or computer-based, although all current discusison, including ours, focus on computer-supported application, provides the primary terminology one need for understanding the present uses of computers as decision and control tools in organization.

   There is no agreement on the term "Management Information System." Some writers prefer term as such as "Information Processing System", others saying "information/decision system," or computer-based information processing systems which are designed to support the operations and management functions of an organization.

5. Management Information System (MIS) is a system designed to supply information required for effective management of an organization. Any organization is managed by taking various decisions at the various levels of its management hierarchy. Information is needed to take these decisions. Quality of decisions will largely depend upon the nature and type of information provided for taking the decisions. Therefore, designing of an effective information system is vital for the efficient working of an organization. It can be built around electronic computers in case of a big organization.

6. Management Information System is designed to supply

information required for effective management of an organization. Any enterprise is managed by means of a variety of decisions made at various levels of its hierarchy. Information is needed to make these decisions. Quality of decisions will largely depend on the nature and quality of information provided for making the decisions. Thus, provision of an adequate information system is vital for the effective functioning of an organization.[1]

Moreover, management information system is both a management system and an information system. Thus unlike data bank information systems or information retrieval systems, where the system's capabilities for providing information may be an end in itself.

7. The management information system (MIS) is a variety of information system which is specifically designed to support decision-making and action.[2]

Murdick and Ross[3], says that 8. Management Information System designed to take advantage of modern tools and technique. MIS is neither refers to a traditionally data processing nor to the sophisticated computer system. 9. The objective of an MIS is to provide information for keeping control over the operations of the sub-systems of the firm and to provide a synergistic organization in the process.

Carl Hayel says 10. "MIS are planned and organized approaches to supply executive with intelligence aids that facilitate the managerial process. It refers to a continuing system and a system to establish for one-time reports. The system may but need not involve the use of electronic data processing equipment and this system can be manual or computer based.

From the analysis of the above views, one can infere that the 11. MIS is a systematic approach to furnish timely, adequate accurate information to the proper persons in the hierarchy with a view to assist him in taking decision.

An Adelberg defines 12. "Management Information System as executive function of planning organising, co-ordinating, directing, controlling and supervising an industrial or business project or activity with responsibility for results." Information is defined as the 'communication or reception of knowledge for intelligence.' A system is defined as a complex unity, formed of many diverse parts subject to a common plan or servicing a common purpose.[4]

Thus an 13. MIS can be thought of as a vehicle designed to integrate data collection accumulation, summarisation and analysis on a timely basis to aid management in planning, organizing, co-ordinating, supervising, and controlling any and all business activities.[5]

The above noted deprivation gives more emphasis in the following points:

(i) determination of what kinds of data, in terms of both quality and quantity, are required by corporate management;

(ii) accumulation of that data in as meaningful, useful and simplified a manner as is reasonable;

(iii) communication of that data on a timely basis to management so that intellegent decision-making results.

According to John Dearden Management Information System 14. (MIS) is a combination of people, machines and procedures organized to provide "past, present and projection information relating to internal operations and external intelligence". 15. It supports the planning, control and operational function of an organization by furnishing uniform information in the proper time frame to assist the decision-making process.[6] This operational definition clearly express how an MIS operates. The source has been discussed below:

1. *Real-time*: A real-time MIS is one which updates data continuously and provides information immediately upon request.
2. *On-line*: Persons, equipment, or device that are in direct communication with the central processing unit of a computer.
3. *Off-line*: Persons, equipment, or devices not in direct communication with the central processing unit of a computer.
4. *Feedback*: Result is compared with plan, an inference initiates an action to bring result closer to plan.[7]

In other words it is an information system using formalised procedures to provide managers at all levels in all functions with appropriate information from all relevant sources (both internal and external to the firm) to enable them to make timely and effective decisions for planning, directing and controlling the activities for which they are reponsible. It will be noted from this definition that the emphasis is on the uses of which the information is put and that no mention is made of the means by which the information is processed. This emphasis is correct for it is the end use of the information which is important and not the intermediate processing stage.[8]

Management Information System (MIS)—A Formal Approach

Stoner and Wankel have defined 16. MIS "as a formal method of making available to management the accurate and timely information necessary to facilitate the decision-making process and enable the organizations' planning. Control and operational functions to be carried out effectively."[9] 17. The system provides information to the management on relevant events (past or present including projects for the future. The information may be made available from within the organization or from outside sources.

The use of the word "formal" in our definition is not intended to negate the importance of the informal communication network in the organization' control mechanism. In fact, managers often detect problems before they show up in formal control reports because they are tuned in to the grapevine.[10]

Furthermore, 18. MIS is a formal system in the business which provides management with the necessary reports to be utilized in the decision-making process. Every manager has to take various decisions from time to time which are in the best interest of the objectives of the organization utilized in the decision-making process. Every manager has to take various decisions from time to time which are in the best interest of the objectives of the organization as a whole. For performing this role, they need specific elements of information. Which may emerges from internal environment in the organization and external environment round the organization.

The following chart shows the information system process:

Review of Literature on MIS Indian Experience

Subhash Sharma[11] (1985) has mentioned in his paper that "the basic objective of management control is to modulate the goal directed behaviour of the organizations". Therefore, the control systems and in particular MIS aims as measurement of the performance againt predetermined standard so that the behaviour of the organization can be properly monitored. In order to know whether the organization is moving in the right direction, it would be necessary for the management to know the direction of movement through proper signals. Furthermore, MIS should aim at focussing the attention of managers on the key variables. Hence, one of the important design consideration is that MIS should highlight the key

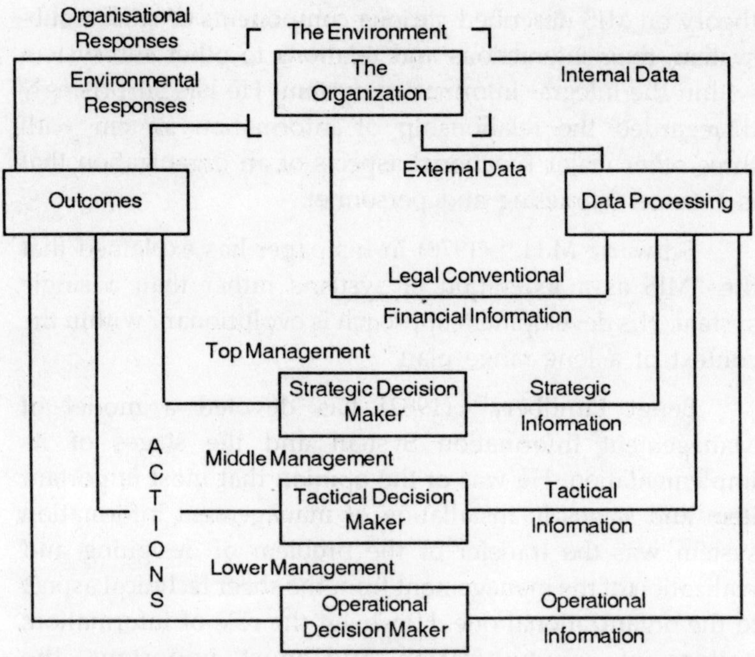

Source: Sherlekar, S.A. and Sherlekar U.S., *Principles & Practice of Management*, 1995, pp. 435-440.

variables. He has also explained some of the key variables related to input which are raw material availability. Quality, raw material costs, capacity, losses, quality control, maintenance, marketing variables, market share, order book position and environmental variables.

Narendra K. Shethi[12] in his article has stated that the "MIS is simply available that has been put on an activity that goes in on every organization—the formalized marshalling of information to support the decision-making process". Every organization has an information system; manual of combination of man and machine; good, bad or indifferent.

Review of Literature on Management Information System —Abroad

Simat M.[13] (1973) has stated that management information system should be linked with the manufacturing activity. His theory on MIS described various components of such a sub-system, their interactions and relations to other sub-system within the integral information system. He has surprisingly disregarded the relationship of information system with three other major functional aspects of an organization that is finance, marketing and personnel.

Schwartz M.H.[14] (1970) in his paper has explained that the "MIS as a federation of systems rather than a single system. His development approach is evolutionary within the context of a long-range plan".

Bengt Lundbery[15] (1982) has devoted a model of Management Information System and the stages of its implementation. He was of the opinion that most important item and stages in installation of management information system was the transfer of the problem of designing and realization of the management from the sheer technical aspect to the organizational one. However, the role of information, pattern of communication and most important—the information content has not been highlight.

Ehrlemark[16] (1984) in his article "Design your own Management Information System" presented a set of conceptual tools to help management design control systems that are sensitive to changes and identify the problems and possibilities for action. Here, the stress has been more on the physical structure of the organization.

Objectives of MIS

The objective of MIS is to provide information for decreases making the planning, initiating, organizing and controlling the operation of the sub-systems of the form and to provide a synergistic organization in the process. Some of the common objectives of MIS found in various enterprises are listed below:

1. To make the desired information available in the right form the person and at the right time.

2. To measure the information from all sources.
3. To identify relevant information and offer to manager for decision-making/problem solving.
4. To supply the required information at a reasonable cost.
5. To use the most efficient methods of processing data.
6. To provide necessary security and secrecy for important and confidential information for decision-making.
7. To keep the information up-to-date.
8. To provide current and future information on administration production, marketing, research facilities.
9. To raise managing from the level of piecemeal spotty information, intuitive guesswork, and isolated problem-solving to the level of systems insights, systems information, sophisticated data processing, and systems problem-solving.
10. To provide a system of information as a powerful method of aiding managers in solving problems and making decisions.

Functions of MIS

All the managerial functions such as planning, organizing directing and controlling are necessary for successful organizational performance. To support these functions, especially planning and controlling, system supplying information to managers are of special importance. Only with accurate and timely information can manager monitor progress towards their goals and turn plans into reality. If managers cannot stay "on track", anticipating potential, corrections, developing the skills to recognize when corrections are necessary, and then making appropriate corrections of adjustments as they progress, their work may be both fruitless and costly.[17]

MIS is an organized way of sending, receiving and recording messages. It includes both formal flow of information as well as informal flow of information, called grapevine. Ideally, information should be accurate, adequate, up-to-date, reliable, timely and understandable. In our system of information there should be no overlaps, no gaps and no contradictions.

The basic function of MIS is to gather data on various aspects of the operation, accounting, statistical and others; process the data using statistical and operations research techniques; and present the summary and display of this information to the management. The application of MIS range from pay-roll and management. The application of MIS range from pay-roll and billing (EDP functions which are purely classical in nature) to information processing for business decisions using "big brain" data basis, to store the data and information on all operations of the company. The overall management information system can retrieve and analyze relevant data required for decision-making.[18]

Elements of MIS

The MIS can be subdivided into four categories each type of system is designed to cater to a specific requirement. The types are:

(i) *Transaction Processing System*: These systems are designed for processing day to day transactions occurring in the organization. These systems involves large volume of data and mainly help in the operation control area of the company.

(ii) *Information Providing System:* Attempt is made here to generate information to help decision-making activity. Starting with transaction processing system summary and exception reports are produced. Summary reports are tabulation of detail by categories. Exception reports provide information about deviations of actuals from planned and indicate the reasons of deviations.

(iii) *Decision Support System:* This system is for improving the analytical capability of the decision-maker. Attempt to made here to create an interactive model of a real life situation, so that the decision-maker can interrogate the system for generation and evaluation of various alternatives.

(iv) *Programmed Decision Making System:* This involve creating systems for programmed decision areas, so that a decision is made by the system instead of a person. This required very clear specifications of the procedure used.

2. Factors Influencing the Value of MIS

The value of MIS is defined in terms of how much benefit can accrue to the organization through its use. The greater the benefit, the more valuable the information. Four primary factors determine the value of information: (i) Information appropriateness (ii) Information quality, (iii) Information timeliness, and (iv) Information quantity. If these attributes are found in the information made available to the persons, real and appropriate decisions can be taken in time and if there is any variation from the standards set as per the decision, acroactive action can be immediately taken. In general, management should encourage the generation, distribution, and use of organizational information that is appropriate of high quality, timely and of sufficient quantity.

MIS is also known as 'Informatics'. Informatic is the science concerned with the collection, transmission, storage, processing and display of information,[19] and information is a tangible or intangible entity that serves to reduce uncertainty about some state or event.[20]

Value of MIS

It must be realized that an MIS has no intrinsic value of its own. It cannot be emphasized too strongly that the value of an MIS can only come from the users of the system, and not from the producers of the information. The users, i.e. management at all levels and functions, can only cause value to be attributed to the MIS as a result of actions following decisions taken using the information provided. The values which may be imputed to any MIS can only come from actions which a. Increase profits, b. Reduce costs, c. Utilize resources more effectively or in some way increase the present or future efficiency of the organization.

Factors Influencing Structure of MIS

Numerous factors influence the overall structure of MIS the more important ones being:

(a) *The primary function of the organization*. It is manufacturing company, a wholesaler, a public authority etc.?

(b) *The structure and levels of the organization*. Is the organization composed of numerous sections and levels? What degree of autonomy have the section/departments?

(c) *The degree of centralization or decentralization*. Is the organization tightly controlled at the centre? What decisions/actions are the sections allowed to take?

(d) *Interaction with environment*. To what extent is external information of importance? In what ways does the organization need to communicate with environment—to customers, suppliers, trade unions, government departments, etc.?

(e) *What decisions need to be taken*. What is the extent of programmed and non-programmed decision-making?

What levels take the decisions? What is the urgency surrounding the decision making process?

(f) *The scale of operation.* How many employees? How many branches/departments/sections? What is the volume of orders, invoices, bills, enquiries, transactions etc.?

(g) *The management style?* Is it an authoritarian or participative style? Are procedures and operations routine and closely prescribed? Is management by exception practised?

Impact of MIS upon the Organization

Impact of MIS upon the organization can be viewed separately with respect to the organizational structure and the individual. Typical changes of reorganization of departments, changes in tasks and changes in communication channels affect the degree of centralization. MIS, rather than leading to centralization, appears to be a neutral element, which will be fitted into the basic managerial philosophy of the organization. Indeed, it is quite likely that there will be centralization of computer facilities, with an accompanying decentralization of managerial decision-making. Centralization of facilities because of cost advantages and decentralization of managerial decision-making because of complexity of organizations. This type of decision-making is frequently determined not by the MIS, but the personal preferences or philosophies of the chief executive.[21]

In a rather detailed study, it was found that in a company with a centralized decision-making philosophy a physically centralized computer works best, while on with a centralized decision-making philosophy obtains better results with a decentralized computer system. The overall managers of the computer was found to be centralization in 30 out of 33 firms, while the managers philosophy of the firms determined the extend to which systems and planning and computer operations aspects of the computer organizational structure would be centralized.[22]

The trend survey conducted by Hunt and Newelz[23] indicates that contrary to a football and bell-shaped organizational structure predicted by Leavitt and Whilser the conventional pyramid is likely to continue.

Establishment of a MIS can affect the distribution of power within the organization. One department can provide another with more accurate information, thereby reducing the latter department's uncertainty. This gives the former department leverage over the latter. Creation of a separate data processing department may cause difficulty in replacing such department thereby giving them more lower in their actions. Since there is more information flow capability with MIS, the importance and degree of inter-dependence of department are increased when compared with a structure manual information system. These impacts on MIS are not much different from similar impacts on other information systems, specifically a manual system.[24]

Management Information System—Planning Framework

Missing, delayed, irrelevant or inaccurate information generally results in erroneous decisions and opportunity losses. Costs of acquiring and processing information are high.[25] The planning process of an organization is dependent upon information, its success, a function of the timeliness, accuracy and relevancy of the information. Zani's[26] "Blueprint" for MIS provide a good top-down approach to MIS design. He argues that most management information systems have spun off as by products of operational and automated clerient systems rather than being design specifically to support the manager in his decision-making activity. He puts forth a comprehensive framework for planning and implementing management information systems from the top-down approach. MIS planning must be made within the context of the corporate planning framework. A company strategy is a blend of internal company resources with external forces—market opportunities, risks, and competitive activities. The internal strategy then determines organizational structure and also the practical strategy for augmenting the company's resources with new ones, via short and long-range planning, internal sources, external forces, strategy and organization structure are the key success variable of a company.

Preliminary Planning Decision Analysis Model

A preliminary planning decision analysis model, on the form of a series of questions, should be utilized to help isolate the specific information requirements for these decisions: (1) What decisions are made? (2) What decisions need to be made? (3) What factors are important in making these decisions? (4) How and when should these decisions be made? (5) What information is useful in making these decisions?

The decision-analysis section is divided into three segments—operational control, strategic planning decisions and management control. It is particularly important and useful to recognize these three distinct sub-processes of management information system design because each requires different types of information and analysis.

Operational Control

Within the operational control for example, many decisions can be programmed—that is, one can build a program that identifies the time at which a decision is needed,the alternatives available, and the criteria for selecting the best alternative under different circumstances.

Strategic Planning

Within strategic planning, on the other hand, it is frequently extremely difficult to determine when a decision is needed, and developing alternative solutions to a problem of strategic planning. It is a creative process that cannot be predefined or prescribed. Hence, the kinds of information and analysis needed for strategic planning are quite different from the kinds needed for operational control. Decision analysis should filter information requirements for the appropriate management sub-process. Therefore, this framework makes explicit that: (1) Objectives dictated by strategy, (2) Specific tasks and their interrelationships, displayed via organizational structure, (3) Key success variables. Using these elements as a base, an analysis of a company's decision-making patterns in strategy, managerial control, and operational control provides the specific information requirements for the critical areas of company operations. It is by identifying these factors and guiding their analysis that managers make their contributions to MIS development.

Schwartz[27] advocates a highly systematic approach to MIS planning. He views MIS as a federation of systems rather than a single system. His development approach is evolutionary within the context of a long-range plan. "The real planning roles of the experts are one to bring disciplines, structure and articulation to user expressions of problems needs are objectives and second to provide for reasonable consideration of technologies potentials and problems."[28]

Types of Management Information Systems

The top level of management needs to make projections and give directions for work. The system required at their level is Executive Support System (ESS), which provides them with the aggregate of internal/external data in the form of graphics, simulations etc. At the middle level, managers need to direct and control the working of all operations as per directions of the top management. Thus, they need systems which provide fast communication in either direction and help accumulate data in concise and presentable formats. This is provided by Office Automation Systems (OAS) and

Management Reporting Systems (MRS). Middle managers also need to make prompt decisions based on some business/ mathematical models. This is facilitated by Decision Support Systems (DSS). At the lower level, "workers take care of day-to-day transactions." They handle the large volumes of data. Thus, Transaction Processing Systems (TPS) offer them a better way of handling data volumes efficiently.

Benefits of Management Information Systems

1. *Operational Efficiency*: It refers to doing things right, better, faster or cheaper. For example, using machines to handle all the accounting transactions of a large manufacturing company would save the need of numerous clerks required and would reduce the time required to handle volumes of data as compared to the manual system requirements.

2. *Functional Effectiveness*: Whereas Efficiency relate to doing things right, effectiveness relates to doing the right things, e.g. the introduction of a DSS leads to better decision-making by a manager, thus, making him more effective in his job. For instance, reduction of bad debts, scrap material, losses, or product development cycle are indications of effectiveness. It is important to determine the effectiveness of a system, but it is relatively tough to measure such an intangible parameter. No discrete methods are available for this.

3. *Quality Customer Service*: This is, perhaps, the most affected area in any business by the developments in IS. The service industry, e.g., Travel Agents, Hotel, Banking etc. has been reshaped by the availability of current technology, e.g., ATMs (Automatic Teller Machines) enable bank depositors to withdraw money 24 hours a day, 7 days a week. This has led to operational efficiency as well as functional effectiveness.

4. *Product Development*: The development, manufacturing and distribution of products has also been assisted by information technology. Engineering and drafting tasks are simplified by Computer Aided Design (CAD) and Computer Aided Engineering (CAE). Robitics and Artificial Intelligence, MRP (Material Resource Planning) systems, Computer Aided Manufacturing (CAM) and many packages for purchase, distribution etc. are making flexible manufacturing systems (FMS) and computer-integrated manufacturing (CIM) possible to implement.

5. *Identifying Business Opportunities*: In a fast growing business environment, taking advantage of shorter product life-cycle, exploiting niche markets are the keys to success. Under such conditions, the computer is an ideal tool for spotting subtle changes or trends in the environment which, otherwise, are beyond a human capacity to perceive, e.g. many stock brokers or financial officers use computers to track stocks and decide on buying or selling accordingly.

6. *Client Lock-In/Competitor Lock-Out*: The customers always get benefit from a coordinated effort for improving information systems, e.g., the travel agents who get terminals from American Airlines get closer to the Airlines. Similarly, other competitors feel knocked out as one company finds an extra edge in technology to lock in the clients.

7. *Inter-Organizational Linkages and Electronic Markets*: Systems that link a company to its customers, distributors, or suppliers are termed inter-organizational systems as they automate the flow of information across organisational boundaries. They allow processing capabilities of one organisation to improve the performance of another or to improve to inter-relations. In addition to providing tight linkages to fix prices

separately. This way, they create an electronic market. Internet facilitates electronic marketing.

Requirements for a Successful MIS

The objective of a MIS is to provide information for decision-making planning, organizing and contributing the operations of the sub-system of the firm and to provide a synergistic organisation in the process. Looking at various studies made to identify parameters responsible for successful information system projects the following key factors can be identified:

- — Involvement of top management in the development of information systems.
- — Active participation of operating management.
- — User satisfaction to be used as the evaluation criterion for information systems.

A new system, when introduced, produces newly emerging behavioural patterns which are not likely to match the theoretical required organizational patterns. These emerging behavioural patterns are the ones that translate system inputs into system outputs. However, therefore the 'required' organisational patterns must be modified to build upon the positive potential of the behavioural aspects. People must see in the MIS features that support their social and psychological needs.

There are two common approaches for development of MIS. Bottom-up approach and Top-down approach. In Bottom-up Approach, initially the transaction processing modules are created and later models for planning, control, strategic planning etc. are added. The system grows in response to the increased needs of the users.

Thus bottom-up approach starts with the existing computer system and the system architect is buffered from linking informational requirements to key management decisions and linking these decisions to organisational objectives, the control of the MIS design in this case is indirect. Usually in practice, a mix of the two approaches is used.

In bottom-up approach the system grows in response to the real needs of users, the main disadvantage is that integration or synthesis of various modules may not be done efficiently and might turnout to be very costly. Various sub-systems may need to be redesigned due to the changing requirements and new interfaces with other subsystems.

REFERENCES

1. Chhabra, T.N., *Principles and Practice of Management*, Dhanpat Rai & Sons, New Delhi, 1991, p. 577.
2. William, R. King, *Marketing Management Information System*, Petrocelli-Charter, New York, 1977, p. 13.
3. Murdick and Ross, *Information System for Modern Management*, Prentice Hall of India Private Ltd., 2nd Edition, New Delhi, 1977, p. 6.
4. Adelberg, A.H., "MIS & Their Implication", *Management Account*, Vol. 53, Delhi, October 1975, p. 320.
5. *Ibid.*, p. 320.
6. John Dearden, "MIS is a Mirage", *Harvard Business Review*, January-Feb., 1978, p. 91.
7. *Ibid.*
8. Davis, G.B, *MIS: Conceptual,—Foundations,—Structure and Development*, International Student Edition, Delhi, 1974.
9. Puri, G.K., *Principles of Management for All*, IIMS Publications, New Delhi, 1996, p. 321.
10. Stoner, J.A. & Freeman, R.E., *Management*, Prentice Hall of India Private Ltd., Second Edition, New Delhi, 1992, p. 670.
11. Subhash Sharma, "Key Variables and MIS Design", *Economic Times*, New Delhi, October, 1985.
12. Narendra K. Sethi, "MIS and Planning Interface", *Integrated Management*, May 1980, pp. 30-44.

13. Simat, M., "Opportunities to Construct a Productions Management in Promotion System for Manufacturing Organization", *Informatologica Yogoslavica*, Vol. 5 (1/4), Yogoslavia, 1973, p. 23.
14. Schwartz, M.H., "MIS Planning" *Datomation*, September, 1, 1970, pp. 28-31.
15. Bengt Lundbery, "On Corrections of Information Models", Sweden, 1982.
16. Ehrlemark, U., "Design Your Own Management Information System in Long Range Planning", Vol. 17(2), Sweden, April 1984, pp. 85-95.
17. Chhabra, T.N., *Principles & Practice of Management*, Dhanpat Rai & Sons, Delhi, 1991, p. 578.
18. Robbins, S.P., *Management Concepts & Applications*, Prentice Hall, New Jersey, IInd Edition, 1987, p. 501.
19. Sherlekar, S.A. & S.A. Sherlekar, *Principles of Business Management*, Himalaya Publishing House, New Delhi, 1995, p. 445. 20.
20. Samuel, C. Certo, *Principles of Modern Management—Functions and Systems*, 3rd Edition, M.C. Brown Publishers Dubugue, Lowa, 1985.
21. Dennis Longley & Michael Shain, *Dictionary of Information Technology*, 2nd Edition, Oxford University Press, 1987, p. 63.
22. Henry, C.Lucas, *Information Systems Concepts for Management*, 1984, p. 1.
23. John, Diebold, "What's Ahead in Information Technology", *Harvard Business Review* (Sept.-Oct. 1965), p. 82.
24. Neal, J. Dean and James, W. Taylor, "Managing to Manage the Computer", *Harvard Business Review* (Sept.-Oct. 1966), pp. 104, 105, 109.
25. Shethi, N.K., "MIS & Planning Interface", *Integrated Management*, May, 1980, p. 714.
26. *Ibid.*, p. 714.
27. William, M. Zani, "Blueprint for MIS", *Harvard Business Review*, November-December, 1970, pp. 95-100.
28. Schwartz, M.H., "MIS Planning", *Datomation*, September 1, 1970, pp. 23-31.

6

Management Information System and Decision-Making

Successful Business operation depends on successful decision-making. Successful decision-making is based on information. Decision-making is an important part of the managerial task and takes place at all levels. In general the life of manager is filled with making decision after decisions. Managers see decision-making as their central job because they constantly decide what is to be done? Who is to do? When, where and how to do? The management functions such as formulating plans, establishing objectives, laying down policies, and so on are the most important decisions made by groups of managers rather than by an individual.[1]

The ultimate purpose of MIS is to make decision at all levels of operations based upon the information flow. The higher level of management is concerned with external factors such as new and proposed government legislation, changes in the market, the state of the economy, the action of competitions, etc. At lower levels, external influences are if considerable less important. Information is the essential ingredient of management and decision-making. A value of information can be computed for decisions, which fits these Frameworks of analysis.[2]

Thus, managerial decisions are based on the flow of information. The decision is the point at which plans, policies and objectives are translated into concrete actions. Planning leads to sound decision-making and implies decision-making, i.e. the selection, from among alternatives, of a course of action. In other words, decision-making is at the core of planning. For instance, choosing of objectives, policies, procedures, programmes, rules, strategies and tactics etc., needs the entire process of decision-making. Therefore, the quality of managerial decision is linked with the quality, quantity, adequacy and speedy availability of data.[3] The purpose of decision-making as well as a planning is to direct human behaviour and effort towards a future goal or objective. After all, it is on the processes of planning/controlling that most decision-making is done.

In the entire process of management and in each of the management activities, such as planning, organizing, leading, controlling, etc., decision-making is always essential.[4] Managerial function is exercised through decision-making. Decision is necessary on numerous issues and problems in each areas of business, e.g., production, marketing, finance, personnel, administration, etc. hence, decision-making process is at the centre of the management universe. A manager reaps a double advantage when he faces a problem and has to find a sound solution. Firstly, he serves the organization when he successfully overcomes the obstacle. Secondly, he achieves simultaneously personal satisfaction and advancement—a sense of accomplishment which is the best reward to satisfy egoistic demands. As decision-making spreads through all elements of management, many a time, management is defined as decision-making process. Whatever a manager does, he doess through a decision-making to make a judgement regarding what one ought to do in a certain situation after considering thoroughly the available alternative course of action.[5]

Decision-making always involves a choice between alternatives and always involves risk as it is concerned with estimates of future revenues, costs, outcomes and events, none of which can be known with certainly. Information reduces uncertainly and helps manager to see the likely effects of various decisions but the information system does not make the actual decisions—that is a MIS function. The function of MIS is to provide decision-makers with timely and accurate data to allow to make and implement the necessary decisions to optimise the interrelationships of men, materials, machines, and money to most effectively reach the organizations predetermined goals.

Meaning of Decision-Making

Decision-making is a conscious human process. The verbs 'decide' is derived from the Latin Prefix 'de' meaning 'off' and the word 'caedo' meaning 'to cut'. In this sense some cognitive process cuts off as preferred, or selects, a particular course of action from among a set of possible alternatives. To decide means to come to a conclusion or resolution. F.A. Shull[6] and others have defined decision-making as the "conscious and human process, involving both individual and social phenomenon based upon factual and value premises, which concludes with a choice of one behavioural activity from among one or more alternatives with the intention of moving toward some desired state of affairs". It represents a course of behaviour or action about what must or must not be done. Three aspects of human behaviour are involved in decision-making:

(i) cognition, activities of the mind associated with knowledge;

(ii) the action of the mind implied by such words as willing, desire, and a version, and

(iii) the aspect of the mind associated with emotion, feeling, mood and temperament. All these factors go into decision-making. Thus, decision-making is defined as the selection of the one course of action. It is a choice making activity and the choice determines our action or in action.

Decision-making is the art of determining in one's mind upon an opinion or course of action. According to Donald J. Clough:[7] "the decision-making process involves a problem to be solved, a number of conflicting objectives to be reconciled, a number of possible alternative course of action from which the `best' has to be chosen and some ways of measuring the value or payoff or alternative courses of action".

Thus, the author emphasis that decision-making is the selecting of action from among alternatives to achieve a specific objective or solve specific problem.

Herbert Simon[8] 1977, who won a Nobel Prize for his work on decision-making says that "Management and decision-making are the same thing", Decision-making begins with the recognition of problem, and once it is recognized and defined, alternatives to change the unfavourable situation into a more favourable one are sought.

Decision-making is globally thought to be "selection from alternatives." It is deeply related with all the traditional functions of manager, such as planning, organizing, staffing, directing and controlling. When he performs these functions, he makes decisions. However, the traditional management theorists did not pay much attention to decision-making. In fact, the meaningful analysis of decision-making process was initiated by Chester Bernard (1938) who commented, "The processes of decision are largely techniques for narrowing choice."

The nature of decision-making may be clearly understood by its following characteristic features:

1. Decision-making is an intellectual process that involves imagination, reasoning evaluation, and judgement.
2. It is a selection process in which "best" or most suitable course of action is finalised from among several available alternatives. Such selected alternative

provides utmost help in the achievement of organizational goals. The problems, for which there is only one selection, are not `decision-problems'.

3. Decision-making is a goal-oriented process. Decisions are made to attain certain goals. A decision is rated good to the extent it helps in the accomplishment of objectives.

4. It is a focal point at which plans, policies, objectives, procedures, etc., are translated into concrete actions.

5. Decision-making is a continuous process persuading all organizational activity, at all levels, and in the whole universe. It is a systematic process and an interactive activity.

6. Decision-making involves commitment of resources, direction, or reputation of the enterprise.

7. Decision-making is always related to the place, situation, and time. It may be decision not act, in the given circumstances.

8. After decision-making, it is necessary and significant to communicate its result (decisions) for their successful execution.

9. The effectiveness of decision-making process is enhanced by participation.

Different Theories of Decision-Making[9]

The art of decision-making provide us a variety of approaches, methods and techniques helpful and useful for making high quality of decision. A decision-maker, as an individual, or as a member of formal organization with his own philosophy and perception of the organization, selects for optimising values within the constraints imposed by the organization. Some of these theories are as under:-[10]

1. Probability Theory

Probability is defined as relative frequency. The role played by it in decision-making is that of a substitute for certainty. In an organizational problem where possibility can be substituted for unknowns, the margin of error in the solution is limited.

2. Queuing Theory

Queuing models are used to provide service facilities. It is used to balance the cost of waiting lines verses the cost of preventing waiting lines by increased service. The objective is to minimize the combined cost of queuing delay and service facilities.

3. Liner Programming

This technique is used in finding the solution for optimising an objective function under certain constraints. The technique is concerned with optimum allocation of limited resources for optimising a given function.

4. Game Theory

Game theory is used to determine optimum strategy in a competitive situation, in real life, many business situations involve several competitors, each trying to make use of mathematical techniques combined with logical thinking to evolve the best possible strategy that can beat his competitors.

5. Simulation

In simulation a series of random numbers are generated and stored by a computer. It is a quantitative technique used for evaluating alternatives courses of action based upon facts and assumptions with a computerized mathematical model in order to represent actual decision-making under conditions of uncertainty.

6. Search Theory

This theory concerns itself with search problems. The

problem is characterized by the need for designing a procedure to collect information on the basis of which one or more decisions are made. The theory is useful in places in which some events are unknown to occur but the exact location is not known.

7. Mathematical Decision Theory

It is not designed to show decisions are actually made. Rather, it is design to help the decision maker who is interested in maximising profit in a given situation, to lie out the alternatives in such a way that he sees the risks and the consequences more clearly. With the development of operations research and computers for handling complex mathematical models, this approach is commonly used by large organizations where decision-making problem is very complex.[11]

8. Heuristic Programming

This technique refers to step-by-step search towards an optimum solution when a problem cannot be expressed in mathematical programming form. The method examines successively a series of combinations that lead to stepwise improvement in the solution and the search stops when a near optimum has been found.

9. Value Theory

This theory is considered as a cost reduction technique, which account for a major portion of total cost in most industries by a scientific approach and analysis.

10. Information Theory

This theory is an attempt to formulate a mathematical model for evaluation of information flow within the given organization system.

Types of Decision

There are different types of decision. According to

Drucker, there are four basic criteria, which determine the nature of decision and the level of authority that should decided: There are:

(i) future times involved;

(ii) the qualitative factors;

(iii) whether a decision is rare or routine and repetitive;

(iv) whether the impact of a decision is on other function, areas or on the businessman as a whole.[12]

Decisions are typically characterized as unstructured, semi-structured and structured.

Unstructured Decisions

The unstructured decision involves decision situations where it is not possible or desirable to specify in advance most of the decision procedures to fellow. Many decision situations in the real world are unstructured because they are subjected to too many random or changeable events or involve too many unknown factors or relationships.[13] It is occurs when the relevant parameters as well as the influencing relationships are unknown. The manager does not know the information required. The information system can be of no help to the manager under this type of situation. For unstructured decisions cost system, sales and production R&D planning etc., techniques can be used.

Semi Structured Decisions

Semi-structured decisions occur in an environment where the relevant parameters are mostly known and where influencing relationships are suspected or are approximately known. In such cases the MIS can provide assistance to the decision-maker through provision of information. For semi-structured decisions, e.g. production, scheduling, cash management, overall budget, new product planning, etc., techniques can be used.

Structured Decisions

Structured decisions involve situations where the procedures to follow when a decision is needed can be specified in advance.[14] Structured decisions are those where both the relevant parameters and relationships are known. Any decision process that can be defined in a procedure and issued to any organization is an example of structured process. For example, account receivable inventory control, the reorder point; determination of the economic order quantity, short-term budgeting and the safety stork and stock are structure decision system provides analyses of determination to assist in decision-making. The structured decisions can be automated and can be computerized. The objectives of an MIS is to ensure that all the structured decisions are computer generated and the managers need not spend much time in making structured decisions.

Programmed Decisions

Programmed decisions are applied to structured or routine repetitive problems and for which decision rules and standing procedures can be devised.[15] Programmed decision may involve considerable amounts of money so came must be taken to ensure that procedure are appropriate. A typical programmed decision is stock re-ordering with calculated reorder levels and reorder quantitative or reorderingof standard inventory item represents programmed decisions based on standard inventory models. Now-a-days programmed decisions are made through management information system is computer based.

Programmed decisions are decisions that can be pre-specified by a set of rules or decision procedures. Programmed decisions can presumably be handled by a computer program since the rules for arriving at a decision are completely defined and only the values of variables must wait for the specific problem. In addition to a computer program, other examples of methods of implementing programmed decision are decision rulebooks, decision tables, and regulation. These programmed decision methods imply a closed decision model because all outcomes and consequences must be known.[16]

Non-programmed Decisions

Non-programmed decisions are used for unstructured, unique, ill-defined situations of a non-recurring nature. They are non-repetitive decision often with high levels of risk where many factors from inside and outside the organization have to be considered. They are handle by general problem solving processes. They involve judgement, intuition and creativity. They are made by trained and higher level manager. Non-programmed decisions are one-time or recurring decisions that which change each time they are required. Decisions in open decision system are non-programmed.[17]

Relationship between Programmed and Non-Programmed Decision-Making

Programs are simply a string of instructions to accomplish an assignment. The concept of programmed decisions is important because the ultimate goal of information systems is to provide purely programmed decision. If this is not possible, we seek to provide the optimum type of information to the human decision-maker, who than makes non-programmed decisions. Decisions are non-programmed if they are unstructured, of high consequences or complex or involve major commitments. Decisions that cannot be automated are also called non-programmed decisions. One of the goals then of MIS design is to device decision rules for the problems that lend themselves to solution by decision rules and the programmed approach.

In order to develop effective programmed decision, the decision-maker must develop a set of decision rules. For example, if MIS is used for inventory control, the re-ordering of item can be programmed. Since the MIS keeps complete a accounting of inventory levels of any given item, a decision rule could be devised such that computer will recommend re-ordering as soon as the inventory level falls below X units (reorder point). The Economic Order Quantity (EOQ) and re-order point can be determined by analyzing the inventory environment and constructing an inventory model to replicate the decision situation. Another example of programmed decision is one of blending various food or chemical ingredients to produce amounts of outputs to meet demands subject to input resources availabilities. A linear programming model can be used to implement these decisions.

Programmed and Non-Programmed Decision-Making Chart

The useful and well known model proposed by Herbert A Simon will be used as the basis for describing the decision making process. Every decision is outcome of a dynamic process, which is influenced by multiple forces. This process is presented in Figure-I.

Classification of Decision	Decision Making	
	Old	New
Programmed Repetitive and Routine	Habit Standard operating Procedure Organization Structure Policy etc.	Management Information System (including Management Science Techniques and The Computer)
Non-Programmed One-shot, ill-structured	Judgement, intuition Insight Experience Training and Learning	Systematic approach to Problem-solving & Decision-making

Fig. 6.1 *Chart shows the Programmed & Non-Programmed Decisions*

Source: Murdick R.G. Ross J.E. and Gloggen J.R. "Information Systems for Modern Management" Prentice Hall of India Private Limited, Third Edition, New Delhi, 1995, p. 190.

Strategic Decision

A strategic decision is one which is made during a current time period but whose primary effect will be felt during some future time period. Strategic decisions affect organizational structure and objectives. Strategic decision cannot be delegated lower than a particular level.[18]

Tactical Decision

Tactical decisions are tactical in nature and also called, routine decision. They are important repetitive need little thoughts with few alternatives. The decision are taken up by middle and first line managers and do not involve any higher risk or uncertainty. Tactical decisions support and compliment organizational strategy. The tactical decision may be delegated to lower levels in the organization. Moreover, what might be strategies decision for one organization may be tactical decision for another.[19]

Organizational Decisions

When a manager acts formally in his expected role in an organization he makes unorganizational decision, which becomes the organization's official decision. Organizational decision reflects company's policies and programmes. They can be delegated to others.[20]

Personal Decision

Personal decisions are made by an executive as an individual and not as a part of the organization. For example, a manager who decides to change his job is making a personal decision. Such a decision does not result in any form of organizational behaviour by others, however, it may affect the organization, but the organization will have to search a replacement for him. Sometimes, it becomes difficult to distinguish between persons and organizational decision. A manager can take a more objective decision when he is convinced that he is talking an organizational decision that which might differ from his personal beliefs. For example, in selecting a salesman for a particular area, the executive may personally feel that local considerations should not weight the decision but from the point of view of organizational effectiveness he may decide to give weightage to the local people. These decisions cannot be delegated.[21]

Decision Making Process

Decision-Making process should not be interpreted to mean that decision-making is a fixed procedure. A process is basically a dynamic concept rather than static. Events and relationships are dynamic, continuous and flexible and must be considered as a whole in which many forces interact: a force affecting others and being affected by others. Therefore, the decision-making process should be seen as sequential process rather than a series of steps to enable decision maker to examine each element in the progression that leads to a decision. Moreover, the process reveals that it is morf applicable to non-programmed decisions than to program ones. Problems that occur in frequently, are unstructured, and are characterized by a great deal of uncertainty regarding their outcome, require the manager to utilize the entire process. For frequently occurring, structured problems, it is not necessary to consider the entire process.[22] The following Fig. shows the decision-making process:

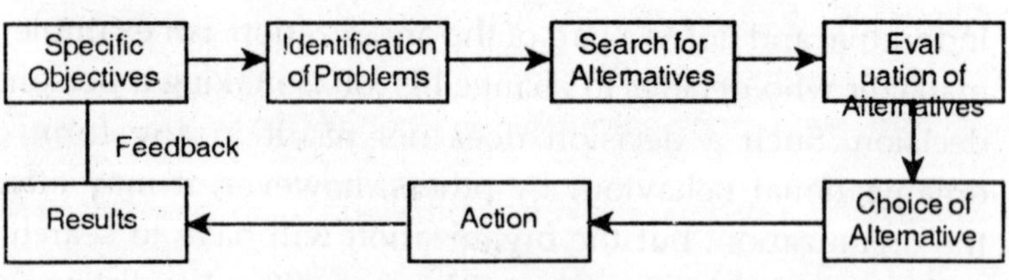

Fig. 6.2 *Decision-Making Process*

Decision-making is a process consisting of logical sequence of interrelated steps, which may be briefly described as follows:

1. Understanding the Background of Specific Objective

Even action of manager should be goal directed to achieve certain specific objective of the organization. Since the objective setting is an outcome of earlier decision, this may not be considered truly as the first step of decision process but concerned with understanding the circumstances surrounding the public of what past action and decision affect the current situation? What objectives and policies impinge as the current decision? What are the key elements in which background that which relate to the public? What is required is intelligent selecting so that relevant background factors are guided with?

2. Problem Identification

Since a particular decision is made in the context of certain given objective. Identification of problem is the real beginning if decision-making process.[23] A problem is a felt need, a question thrown forward for solution. It is the gap between present and desired state of affairs on the subject matter of decision. Further in management, a problem exist whenever one faces a question whose answer involves doubt and uncertainty, if there is no solution to the problem, it cannot be treated as problem from decision point of view, through the consequences of not solving this problem may be terrible. A problem can be identified much clearly, if managers go through diagnosis and analysis of the problem.

The recognition of what is the real problem requires much questioning and thought. For example, a firm is experiencing a drop in sales. What is the problem? Is it the price of the product, the quality, appearance, style, and capability? Is it poor sales and marketing? Is it the lack of advertising or of the right style of advertising, it is the lack of an appropriate incentive scheme for the sales force? Is it the appearance on the market of a superior, competing production? Have the consumers' tastes changes? etc.

3. Search for Alternatives

A problem can be solved in several ways all the ways cannot be equally satisfying. If there is only one way of solving a problem, no question of decision arises. Therefore, the decision maker must try to find out the various alternatives available in order to get the most satisfactory result of a decision. Identification of various alternatives only not serves the purpose of selecting the satisfactory one, but it also avoids bottlenecks in operation, as alternatives are available if a particular decision goes wrong. A decision-maker can use several sources for identifying alternatives: his own past experience, practices followed by other, and using creative techniques. Typical of these are model building and solution, probabilistic analysis, decision trees, cost/volume/profit analysis etc.

4. Evaluation of Alternatives

After the various alternatives are identified, the next step is to evaluate them and select the one that will meet the choice criteria. However, all alternatives available for decision-making will not be taken for detailed evaluation because of the obvious limitations of managers in evaluating all alternatives. Evaluation of various alternatives dissects on alternatives into various tangible and intangible factors. Tangible factors are those which can be quantified because they are quite obvious like the cost per unit, investment required, output to be received etc. as against these, intangible factors are mostly qualitative and cannot be measured in terms of quantity. At this stage the judgment and preferences of the decision maker are of importance. Frequently an optimum solution calculated by a mathematical techniques may not be selected by the decision-maker because of its impact on the organization and some non-optimum but still satisfactory solution would be selected instead. This type of behaviour known as satisficing, appears to be common among decision-makers.

5. Choice of Alternative

In this phase, the person taking the decision selects a particular course of action from those identified in the previous phase or rejects all the alternatives and thus the decision process may be back to the design or intelligence phase.[24]

Management information system is most effective if the results of design are presented in a decision-impelling format. When the choice is made, the role of the MIS changes to the collection of data for later feedback and assessment.[25] In choosing an alternative, the decision maker can go through three approaches experiences, experimentation, and research.

6. Action

Once a decision is taken, its implementation follows: a decision, which is not implemented within a timeframe, is no decision unless it has been superseded, before its implementation, by another decision not to implement it. Most jobs done in an organization involve implementation of decision and should result in performance, achievement of expected results. The basis requirements for any action are: A decision-stored data-work procedure and action information. However, action, whether highly structured or less structured should have a perceptible and tangible outcome. Information that goes into the action process is referred to as 'action information' and is necessarily a part of 'management information'.

7. Results

When the decision is put into action, it brings certain

results. These results must correspond with objectives, the starting point of decision process, if good decision has been made and implemented properly, thus results provide indication whether decision-making and its implementation is proper. Therefore, managers should take up a follow-up action in the light of feedback received from the results. If there is any deviation between objectives and results, this should be analysed and factors responsible for this deviation should be located. Therefore, a successful manager is one who keeps a close look at the objectives and results of the decision and modifies his decision according to the change in the circumstances.

The Systems Concept of Decision-Making

When a system provides information to be used in the managerial decision process, it is called a true information system. An effort is being made to develop such a system that meet the definition of true information system which contains only the information that is pertinent for making decisions and in addition presents it in a meaningful form and available at correct time. The level of information system thus refers to providing the correct input for the management decision process. Stated simply it is providing timely, reliable, and vital information on which to base an effective decision.

The only way to isolate the specific information requirements of individual managers is to isolate the nature, frequency and interrelationships of the major decisions made in the company. One can ask a series of questions, which will help to isolate the specific information requirement for these decisions:-

1. What decisions are made?
2. What decisions need to be made?
3. What factors are important in making these decisions?
4. What information is useful in making these decisions?

Answering all these questions is not possible. But the key success variables analysis. It is essential for an organization that its management develop rational decision-making procedures and strives to improve its decision-making capabilities.

Information Requirement for Decision-Making

Simon[26] has identified following three stages in decision-making:

(i) Intelligence activities concerned with scanning the environment to identify events and conditions requiring decisions. The MIS should contain decisions models to process data and generate alternative solutions. The models should assist in analyzing the alternatives.

(ii) Design phase to develop analyse and evaluate alternative courses of action. This involves processes to understand the problem, to generate solutions, and to test solutions for feasibility.

(iii) Choice implementation activities to select an alternative as appropriate course of action from amongst the available alternatives and implementing and monitoring the alternative selected. The meaning of each phase is summarized in the following chart.[27]

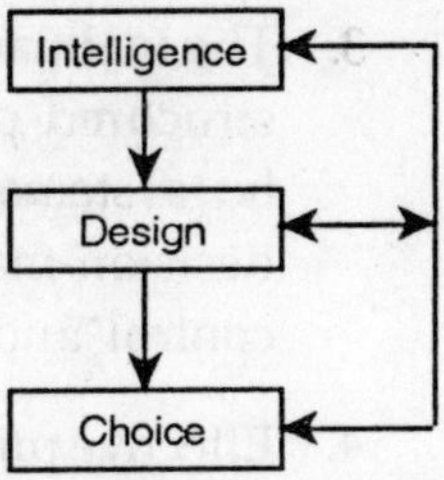

1. Intelligence consists of searching the environment for conditions calling for decisions; it is synonymous with problem recognition.
2. Design is inventing, developing, and analysing possible courses of action.
3. Choice involves selecting a course of action and implementing it.

Decision Support System

A decision support system (DSS) is an interactive computer system that is easily accessible to, and operated by noncomputer specialists to assist them in planning and decision-making functions. While DSSs may differ in their emphases on data-access and modeling functions, there is an overriding emphasis in all such systems on user accessibility to data for decision-making.[28] This decision-making applicability permits managers to simulate problems using format mathematical models and to test the outcomes of various alternatives for reaching the best possible decision.[29]

The term decision support system refers to a class of systems, which support the process of making decision DSS allow the decision maker to retrieve data and test alternatives solutions during the process of problem solving. The meaning of DSS is based on following assumptions about the role of the computer in effective decision-making:

1. The DSS must provide case of access to the database containing relevant data and interactive testing of solution.
2. The computer must support the manager but not replace his judgment. It should therefore neither try to provide the answers nor impose a predefined sequence of analysis.
3. The main advantage of computer support is for semi-strucured problems, where parts of the analysis can be systematized for the computer, but where the decision-makers' insight and judgment are needed to control and process.
4. Effective problem solving is interactive and is enhanced by a dialogue between the user and the system. The application of DSS to different types of decisions is shown in Fig.6.3 DSS represent different approach to information system support for semi-structured and

unstructured decision. The approach is not to find a structure and automate it; rather it is to support to variety of unstructured decision process. The choice of DSS is based on the degree of action implication of system outputs that is the degree to which the system output can directly determine the decisions.

Management Activity

	Operational Control	Management Control	Strategic Planning
Structured decision systems — Structured ↑	Inventory reorder decisions, production scheduling	Pricing of bids, selection of credit line institutions	Acquisition of a company addition of new product line
Decision support systems — ↓ Unstructured	Selection of Vendor Hiring of new Super-visor	Allocation of advertising internal organization of department	Entry into new market, new organization of company

Fig. 6.3 *Application of decision support systems to different types of decisions*

Decisions Between DSS and MIS

Since the DSS is an outgrowth of the MIS, there are basic similarities between them. They are both computer-based and designed to supply information to managers.[30] However, there are some important advantages to a DSS. First of all, a DSS is geared to information manipulation and not essentially to data storage and retrieval, as are many MISs.[31] A DSS is operated directly by its users; when they need access to information, they can immediately consult their own on-line system without having to wait days or week for result from the MIS department. Once manager call up the required data through a DSS, they can manipulate it directly, asking questions and reformating the data to meet their specific needs without having to explain what they want to the EDP/MIS staff.[32] Managers can thus be certain that they will get the information they need when they need it. In addition, direct manipulation of data has the advantage of greater security for sensitive information.

Another key difference between an MIS and a DSS is that a DSS helps managers make non-routine decisions in unstructured situations.[33] An MIS, on the other hand, emphasizes standard, periodical reports and cannot respond well to non-routine, unstructured, or adhoc situation.[34] MIS departments may be unfamiliar with the decisions made in such situations; because they often have a tremendous backlog of requests for data they may be unable to respond quickly to additional special requests. Conversely, some managers who have no difficulty manipulating the data.

Decision-Making and MIS

An MIS is a processor of information to yield decision. The quality, quantity, rate of flow, and timing of information supplied by the MIS to the decision-makers are critical to effective operation of the company. The function of the system within the organization is to evaluate select and manipulate information to decision-makers. Mason has described the process of decision-making consisting of five stages:[35]

1. Source consisting of the physical objects and activities, which are relevant to the business.
2. Data-observation, measurement and recording of data from the source.
3. Inferences and predictions drawn from the source.
4. Values and choice evaluation of interferences with regard to values of the organization and choosing a course of action.
5. Action talking of course of action.

As the corporation gains more experience in dealing with their decision problems and develop better understanding about them, the `deep structure' of the decision problem becomes more explicit. The MIS performs three functions with respect to decision-making:[36]

(i) It helps manager to make decisions by supplying needed information and solving optimisation problem for guidance.

(ii) It makes repetitive types of decisions where decision process remains constant but the input varies.

(iii) The quality of information, which is an important factor for the MIS, can be measured by factors like uncertainty clarity, level of detail, accuracy and completeness. The objective of MIS is to provide information according to trade-offs between cost benefits and objectives for these factors for quality. The most valuable combination of MIS is the information it supplies in support of decisions.

Conclusion

Decision-making as the process of selecting an alternative from among several to achieve a set of goals and objectives. To generate and to evaluate, alternative data must be collected, processed and analysed the link between MIS and decision-making is strong and as such they are inseparable in practice. Therefore, the use of quantitative techniques for management decision-making process always involves MIS. The MIS can improve organizational decisions by (a) upgrading the existing clerical system, (b) programming routine decision and (c) providing essential input to non-programmed decision. Of cause, all non-programmed decisions need judgment, experience and intuition in addition to factors and figures. MIS must recognize its limitations in the branch of strategic or unstructured decisions, which involve uncertainty and turbulent environment.

The MIS provides information to assist managers in making decisions. Also it may be designed to provide decision for repetitive classes available to all managers, integrate the management of the company. Thus, the company as a system with oil elements working towards common objectives. Any company that believes that it has genuine management information problems and wants to solve them should consider the following measures:

1. Place efficient and competent people in each of the formal information systems.
2. Examine all the interfaces.
3. Examine the logistics system.
4. Organize a central computer group for systems control.

Thus, MIS is efficient tool providing past, present and projected information relating to internal operations and external intelligence. It supports the planning, control and operaional function in an organization by furnishing uniform information in the proper time frame to assist the decision-maker.

REFERENCES

1. Prasad, L.M., "Principles and Practice of Management", Sultan Chand and Sons, New Delhi, 1997, p. 207.
2. Varma, M.M. and Agarwal, R.K., "Management Information System", King Books, New Delhi, 1998, p. 42.
3. William, R. King, "Marketing Management Information System", Petrocelli/Chater, New York, 1977, p. 5.
4. Tripathi, P.C. & Reddy, P.N., "Principles of Management", Tata McGraw Hill Publishing Company Ltd., Second Edition, New Delhi, 1997, p. 59.
5. Sherleker, S.A. & Sherleker, N.S., "Principles of Business Management", Himalaya Publishing, New Delhi, 1996, p. 79.
6. Fremount, A Shull, Andrew, L. Delbeog & L.L. Cummings, "Organizational Decision Making", McGraw Hill, New York, 1970, p. 31.
7. Donald, C.J., "Concept in Management Science", Prentice Hall of India Pvt. Ltd., New Delhi, 1963.

8. India Management, "Intuitive Decision Making", A Business India Group Publication, Vol. 37, No. 1, January, 1998, p. 89.

9. Varshney, G.K., "Theory and Practice of Management", Top Publication, New Delhi, 1997, p. 178.

10. Patel, R.B., "Management Information System—An Efficient Tool for Decision Making", *Indian Journal of Commerce,* Vol. XL VI, Sept. 1993, pp. 85-86.

11. Varshney, G.K., "Theory and Practice of Management", Top Publication, New Delhi, 1997, p. 183.

12. Nauhria, R.N. Rajnish Prakash, "Management of System", Wheeler Publication, 1st Edition, New Delhi, 1995, p. 771.

13. James, A O'Brien, "Management Information System: A Managerial End User Perspective", Galgotia Publications Private Ltd., 1998, p. 322.

14. *Op. cit.*, Jamees A.O. Brien, p. 321.

15. Robert, G. Murdick, Joel, E. Ross & R. Claggett, "Information Systems for Modern Management", Prentice Hall of India Private Limited, IIIrd Edition, New Delhi, 1995, p. 189.

16. Gordon, B. Davis, "Management Information Systems: Conceptual Foundations, Structure, and Development", International Student Edition, Sydney, 1974, pp. 144-145.

17. *Ibid.*, p. 145.

18. March., J.G., "Decision and Organizations", Cambridge, Massachusetts, Basil Blackwell, 1988.

19. Prasad, L.M., *Principles and Practice of Management*, Sultan Chand & Sons, New Delhi, 1997, p. 208.

20. *Op.cit.*, March, J.G., *Decisions and Organization.*

21. Prasad, L.M., *Principles and Practice of Management*, Sultan Chand & Sons, New Delhi, 1997, p. 208.

22. Prasad, L.M., *Principles and Practice of Management*, Sultan Chand & Sons, New Delhi, 1997, p. 210.

23. Varshney, G.K., *Theory and Practice of Management*, Top Publications, New Delhi, 1997, p. 180.

24. Jagdish, C. Kapur, *MIS: Conceptual and Framework Indian Management*, Indian Institute of Public Administration, New Delhi, 1982, p. 4.

25. Gordan, B. Davis, *MIS; Conceptual, Foundation, Structure, and Development*, International Student Edition, New Delhi, 1974, p. 142.

26. Herbert, A. Simon, *The New Science of Management Decision*, Harper & Brothers, New York, 1960, p. 54.

27. Gordan, B. Davis: *MIS : Conceptual, Foundations, Structure, and Development*, International Student Edition, New Delhi, 1974, p. 319.

28. Steven Alter, in "A Taxonomy of Decision Support Systems", *Sloan Management Review 19*, No. 1 (Fall 1977), pp. 39-59.

29. Bernard C. Reinmann and Allan, D. Waren, "User-Oriented Criteria for the Selection of DSS Software", Communications of the ACM 28, No. 2, (February 1985), pp. 166-179.

30. Stoner, J.A.F. and Freeman, R.E., "Management", Prentice Hall of India Private Ltd., Fifth Edition, 1992, p. 683.

31. "Fourth-Generation Languages Make DSS Feasible for All Managers", *Management Review, 73*, No. 4 (April 1984), pp. 4-5.

32. Donald, R. Wood, "The Personal Computer: How it can Increase Management Productivity", *Financial Executive* 52, No. 2, (1984), p. 15.

33. Andrew, T. Masland, "Integrators and Decision Support System Success in Higher Education", *Research in Higher Education 20*, No. 2 (Feb. 1984), pp. 211-233.

34. Hugh, J. Waston and Marianne, M. Hill, "Decision Support Systems or What Did't Happen with MIS", *Interfaces 13*, No. 5 (October 1983), pp. 81-88.

35. Manson, R.O., "Basic Concepts for Designing MIS", *Managements for Management Decision*, R.O. Mason and E.B. SwiansavAddison Weslay, 1981.

36. Patel, R.B., "Management Information System: An Efficient Tool for Decision-Making", *Indian Journal of Commerce*, Vol. XL VI, Part III, No. 176, September 1993, p. 91.

7

Computer and Management Information System

A decade ago, at the dawn of the computer era, writers of Sunday-supplement articles were of describing the mysterious new electronic gadget as a superbrain possesed of nearly magical powers. More recently it has become fashionable to point out, rather diparagingly, that the computer can do only what it is programmed to do. This sounds a lot more sophisticated, but it misses a crucial point. In the words of Herbert Simon, the observation that the computer can only follow instruction is "intuitively obvious, indubitably true, and supports none of the implications that are commonly drawn from it."[1]

Characteristics of Computer

The characteristic of computer are as follows:

1. The computer is a dutiful and tireless slave in processing huge volumes of paper word—subscriber billing, insurance premium accounting, credit card, invoicing, and so on.

2. It deals with the complete problems.

3. The computer can provide extremely rapid reponse to external event.

4. Computer refers to a device capable of solving

problems by accepting and storing data, performing desired operation on the data and supplying the results of these operations.

5. It is an electronic data processing machine which can receive and store data and perform arithmetical operations on the data at an extremely high speed as per instructions given to it.
6. The computer is a replica of the human brain which can store data and programs in its memory and process the data at a high speed. This process is known as Electronic Data Processing (EDP).
7. The necessary data known as input are fed in a coded form which is processed by the arithmetic unit and the results, known as output, are produced or displayed in the format desired by the operator.[2]

Features of Computer

The most important features of computer are as follows:

1. Mass Storage

A computer can store voluminous data on magnetic tape/magnetic disk because density of recording on magnetic disk is so high that millions or transactions of concerned organization can be recorded and produced any part of it as an when required. A decade or so ago a computer manufacturer announced a memory device that will allow storage demonstration of one million hits per square inch approximately the amount of information on six pages of a four column telephone directory.

2. High Speed

The speed of processing data on computer is incredibility high and can perform millions of operations in seconds. The speed of computer programming expressed in micro-second (1 Micro Seconds = 1/10,00,000 second).

3. Stored Programmes

A computer is capable of storing a set of institutions also known as computer programming and enable computer to switch over from one institution to another automatically without human intervention.

4. Memory

Computer memory specification are no longer stated in micro-seconds last in monoseconds. A nanoseconds—one billionth of a second—is a difficult figure to comprehend, but try this; there are as many nanoseconds in one seconds as there are second in thirty yearss, or as may nanoseconds in 2.5 seconds as there are seconds in a persons life time.

5. Accuracy

In fact, while designing the computer, utmost care is taken to ensure error-free operations. The accuracy in the operations lends reliability to the information generated by the computer. In other words, reliability of information generated through computers depends, to a great extent, on the correctness of the data and instructions fed into the computer.

6. Versatility

Computers are multi-purpose information machines. The same computer can perform the job of a secretary in the morning, work as an accountant during the day, teach the user how to drive a car in the evening, and entertain the user by playing chess with him later in the evening. Such versatility of the computer is possible due to its programmes.[3]

Functions of Computers

The computer performs the following functions:[4]

(i) It receives the programmes of instructions, stores them in its memory and uses them when instructed.

(ii) It serves as a memory of store house of information when asked.

(iii) It performs arithmetical calculations.

(iv) It helps in evaluating various alternative courses of actions.

(v) It can apply checks to the data fed into the computer. It will point out the inconsistencies in the data, if any.

(vi) It arranges information in the required sequence.

MIS

The growth of EDP departments spurred managers to focus more on planning their organizations' information systems. These efforts led to the emergence of the concept of computer-based information systems (CBIS), which became better known as computer-based MIS—or simply MIS. Due to this development the activities of EDP departments grew many fold. There was heavy work load to be coped by EDP departments to meet the growning needs of the operating managers. To meet this challenge of the situation EDP departments developed a standardization of reports. These standardized reports became part and parcel of management information systems.

Role of Computer in Information System[5]

Computer now can take over activities formerly reserved only for the human mind. It can now even think. It can provide brain power. It can hear, see, speak and even sing. The future capacity of computers seems almost unlimited. What the computer cannot do today is make a human value judgment. Hence computerized MIS can only support decision-making when we deal with semi-structured and unstructured decision situations. MIS is best suited for operational planning and control areas particularly in structured or programmed decisions. At the middle and top management level it has only supporting role and can assist in decision-making process. In these areas manager is still the decision-maker. Computer cannot replace manager in semi-structured and unstructured decision areas.

The various sub-systems of MIS collect, process and store necessary pieces of information. This data is stored and maintained in a file (specific space for storage in the computer memory). When the data is needed, the computer software can retrieve it from the file. The collection of such sub-unit files for total organization is called the "central data base" for the MIS. The heart of the MIS is the group of procedures and techniques that retrieve needed information from the central data base, perform necessary analysis and present summary results for review of management. The modern information processing technology offers high-speed, rapid access and mass storage devices to store large amount;of data and information concerning various aspects of the firm and its environment. The information needs of management served by MIS include, for example, forecasting of sales by month or year, master production schedules to meet the forecasted sales, inventory management, plant monitoring and control, purchasing and receiving of raw materials, and exception reports for operations. MIS also provides an effective feedback control mechanism for timely flow of information and imaginative analysis of well chosen information elements which ultimately determine the future of the organization. These three aspects, (1) timely information flow, (2) imaginative analysis and (3) well-chosen information elements, make MIS field exciting, challenging and necessary for organization's survival in the competitive world.

The following Fig. 7.1 shows the function and activities of MIS in organisation.

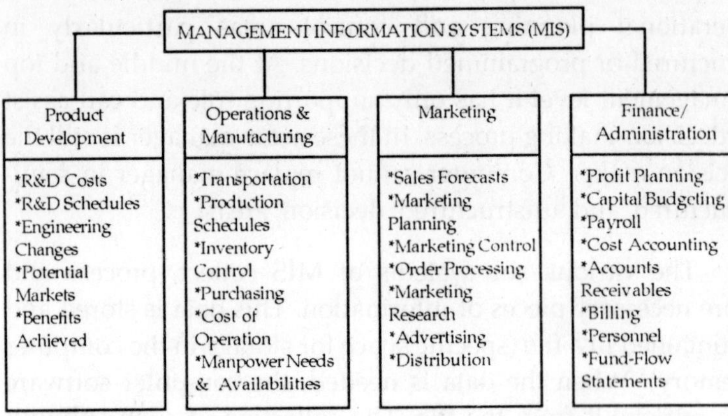

Fig. 7.1 *MIS for Typical Business Organization*

MIS Computer

Computer systems are particularly useful and cost-effective (1) when there is a large volume of routine data to be processed; (2) when tasks and activities are repetitive; (3) when it is necessary to store and have quick access to a large volume of data and information; (4) when speedy processing and up-to-the minute business records are essential; and (5) when there is a need to perform complex computation.

Some experts estimate that more than 50 per cent of managers already use computers daily—a trend that is expected to continue in this millennium, when even routine office jobs will be fully computerized. Thus, current and future managers alike need to become effective at and comfortable with the use of computers and the ways they can: (1) facilitate the collection, management, and communication of information up and down the management hierarchy, as well as between workers on the same level. (2) automate operations, both in the factory and in the office.

(3) support decision making and planning at all levels.
(4) simplify management control.

Management Information System, a discipline of comparatively recent origin (owes) its development to the computer to a great extent. When people in the management field saw the potential of computers for purposes of data storage, processing and retrieval, they went about exploiting this potential for managerial functions. Thus historically, it was the computer that led to the development of MIS as a discipline. True, a manual system of data generation and processing existed in the organizations much before the advent of computers but MIS as a formal discipline was developed only subsequently. No wonder TL Whisler talks of computer as the engine that drive the information technology.[6]

Various authors have described a computer as an essential ingredient of an Information System. James J. O'Brein has stated that an MIS design should be oriented towards computerization since this is inevitable for true MIS. He has further concluded that the development, design and operation of MIS requires a computer. Sherman C. Bluementhal argues for automation of MIS on account of computer's potential for information collection, storage, processing and display.[7] Other authors talk of a computer as the fundamental information processor and the essential element of a Management Information System.[8]

The authorities quoted above are unanimous in adopting a computer-oriented approach towards MIS. Of course, all the authors are from the developed countries where computers became a by word quite some time back. In order to have proper appreciation of this trend, it would be worth while having a glimpse into the historical past. Computers invaded the markets in the developed countries not only on account of their capacity but also because of cheaper cost of operation per unit. Initially computers were used as adjuncts to or replacement for clerical processes such as payroll preparation, inventory reporting, personnel data compilation etc. These operations were essentially of a book-keeping nature. Thus, by the time the concept of MIS was developed, it was only a question of extension of computer usage from book-keeping to personally oriented areas. In other words, disparate use of computers were integrated into larger data collection, processing, retrieval and displays. This was the outline of MIS which got refined further.

Context the process of evolution has not been the same to the extent that MIS had become a familiar discipline even before the usage of computers has gained wide acceptance. There are a large number of organizations where book-keeping operations are being performed manually and this state of affairs is unlikely to change in the foreseable future. Under the circumstances, should we ignore the concept of information based decision-making which is the base of MIS or develop our own mechanics of using this managerial discipline. We can skip the process of evolution by starting with computers specially designed for MIS or we can go ahead with installation of a manually operated information system for as long as it serves the needs of an organization. Resistance to the latter approach is considerable because most of the system designers have had extensive training in the use of computers and their fascination with the machine is generally disproportionate to its raw advantages.

Even while designing a manual MIS, it would be essential to follow a topdown approach, i.e. we will first have to enumerate goals and objectives of an organization, determine various levels of decision-making and asertain their information requirements. Unless this approach is followed, the whole exercise may get reduced to the level of rationalized reports and returns. At this stage we will have to match the information requirements with exiting flow of information so that the objectives can be achieved with minimum disruption. In every organization, some kind of reporting system already exists. It is far easier to mesh this system with a manual MIS compared to an automated system because in the latter case, there is always a temptation to create an information flood merely to ensure optimum utilization of the computer.

Generation of data is done manually in all cases whether it is an automated MIS or an manually one. This data has to be processed in order to convert it into information. There is no getting away this aspect of MIS even a manual system. However, because of its inherent limitation, the manual processing generally takes the form of consolidation summaries or conclusions based on data. If the processing is more complex, we will need a computer. In most organizations, the quantity and variety of data-manipulation or processing is limited and for .such organizations a manual MIS is adequate.

Let us now examine the efficacy of a manual MIS for control functions. In fact MIS is most effective for exercising control in the field of operating sub-systems. This trait is common to the computer-based MIS wherein initial emphasis is on the development of information which is of immediate use to the managers of the sub-systems. Examples of information generation for control purposes are reports on daily production, sales, financial transactions, inventory status, etc. These reports which are used for monitoring can be generated manually unless the mass of data is such that we need a computer. We may also keep in mind the computer output is not always the fastest because computer also depends on inputs and programming. Thus we may find that in some cases a manually operated information sytem has better application for such monitoring and control function than what we might presume.

MIS is also supposed to play a vital role for strategic planning although the extent to which information is actually used for decision-making at the highest level remains doubtful. In USA a survey of 100 top managers of the firms utilizing altogether more than 120 computers had revealed that without exception they made no direct use of the computer for decision-making at the corporate or division level.[9] The investigator who made this survey concluded that only the middle level managers were making use of the computer for decision-making process. May be these middle level managers have been feeding the top management with information-based on computer but there was no direct usage of this information at the top level. We may conclude that in USA middle level managers who mostly exercise managerial and operational control are the major users of the computer. In our case, in the absence of mass production-based technology, such control can legitimately be exercised with the help of a manual MIS in a large area. In some cases, the need for massive information the level of strategic planning is undoubtedly there, but such cases are comparatively few.

In conclusion, it may be stated that certain industries such as Airlines, Railways, large production-oriented units, Banks, etc., need computer for their day-to-day operations but there are sectors such as Government departments, small and medium production units, academic institutions, hospitals, etc. which also need an MIS but can do with a manual system. Also the concept of MIS has changed somewhat in the light of past experience. Earlier senior management had thought of a 'total' corporate information System resembling a Command Information Centre of the Military where there are 'radar-like screens constantly screening the business horison, push-button consoles for instantaneous pulse taking of every corporate artery and immediate communications with every decision and action centre of the business. By now there is widespread recognition that the idealised concept of a total computer based system, embracing an entire business has not been implemented anywhere and may even be impossible has not been implemented anywhere and may even impossible of attainment.[10] The practical difficulties of integrating the information needs of heterogeneous functions of an organization have resulted in shifting the emphasis from total MIS to the so-called sub-systems. This wearing off of the utopia of total MIS augurs well for the manual systems since in the latter case we have to make do with lesser data and the integration of various sub-systems is ruled out.

Evolution of Computer

The history of the computer field is not about people who have been dead for centuries or about events that only historians remember. Many of the key people are still alive and at work. Most of the significant technical developments have occurred so recently that our social systems are still adjusting to them.

The computer was not invented by just one person. It was the product of a long sequence of contributions by a host of people. Let us look at some of the critical events in the development of modern computer systems.

The history of modern day computing begins in the 19th century with the work done by a British mathematician Charles Babbage, he is called the "Father of Computing" because he developed the concepts that underlie all modern computers. Babbage wanted to correct the errors in astronomical tables used for navigation by the British Navy. He thought that a mechanical calculator could do the calculation without error, so he designed the "difference engine". It was to be steam powered and have thousands of gears, wheels and barrels. However, he could never complete the difference engine, partly because the technology of the day could not produce the gears and the wheels with the precision required Babbage later came up with the concept of an "analytical engine" which could do generalized calculations as opposed to the difference engine which could do only one type of calculation.

Herman Hollerith (1860-1926) is credited with the providing impetus for automated data processing. His invention came in response to a problem by the late 1800s it was taking the U.S. Census Bureau more than five years to complete each nationwide census. Hollerith designed and built a sorting and tabulating machine that processed data punched on 80 column cards. Hollerith later resigned his job at the Census Bureau to form his own company which later became International Bussiness Machines (IBM).

One of the earliest electronic computing devices was the ENIAC (Electronic Numerical Integrator and Calculator) which was designed and built at the University of Pennsylvani in the United States. Years of research by a team of scientists led by John Mauchly and Prospor Echort finally culminated in 1946 when the ENIAC started working.

There are many interesting facts about this "giant" computer. It is said to have weighed 30 tons, occupies 1500 square feet of space and had about 18,000 vacuum tubes (valves) in it. Due to the enormous amounts of heat generated by these vaccum tubes, one of them would blow every few minutes. That kept a small group of engineers buy-just replacing blown valves with good ones. Stories about the ENIAC's hunger for power too about. It is said that the lights of Philadelphia city dimmed when the machine was switched on.

The story of ENIAC is interesting for one primary reason. The concept of "generations of computers" begins here. As mentioned earlier ENIAC used vales as its major building block. That is numbers and symbols were manipulate by switching electric current in these valves. Computers which used valves (Much like the radio sets of earlier years came to be known as First Generation Computers).

In the early 1960s the accelerated space research which culminated in man's landing on the moon paved way for the birth of the science of miniaturization. Scientists soon found ways of making "integrated circuits" by closely packing thousands of transistors on a thin water of silicon. Computer designs soon adopted this technology and Third Generation Computers were born.

Today very high levels of integration have been achieved. Latest very large scale integrated (VLSI) circuits have as many as 300,000 circuits embedded on a tiny silver of silicon. Today's computers which use VLSI technology belong to the Fourth Generation.

In early days, computer instructions were given in the machine language—the language of "0"s and "1"s or that of "on"s and "off"s. Each symbol which the computer had to process had to be fed into it in this form. Naturally it was very cumbersome and prone to mistakes. Usage of this first generation software therefore was primarily restricted to research labs.

Soon came the assembly language. Users could now write programs or instructions in a symbolic language. A program called the "Assembler" would then convert these instructions to machine code. Differences however continue. Learning assembly language was very difficult and usage was still restricted to scientific applications. This was the second generation of software.

In the late 1950s, IBM (International Business Machine) now the world's largest computer manufacturer, 1990-91 turn over more than US$ 60 billion introduced a language called FORTRAN, short for FORMA TRANSLATOR, FORTRAN was a "high level" language which used English words and symbols. It was much simpler to learn and use, and was closer to human languages—hence the term high level language. A program called a COMPILER would convert the high level instructions to machine language. Soon compilers for other languages like COBOL, PASCAL, BASIC and C became available. These and other third generation languages are still being used very widely around the world.

However, what has dramatically changed the computing world today is the arrival of easy to use, pre-packaged software which can be fun on inexpensive office computers to solve a staggering variety of common business problems. Some of these are called Fourth Generation Language like dBASE and Spreadsheets.

REFERENCES

1. Herbert Simon, *In the Shape of Automation*, New York, Harper & Row, Publishers, 1965.
2. Hampton, D.R., *Modern Management: Issues & Ideas*, Prentice Hall Pvt. Ltd., Delhi, pp. 189-90.
3. Chhabra, T.N., *Principles and Practice of Management*, Dhanpat Rai & Sons, Fifth Edition, New Delhi, 1991, pp. 583-91.
4. *Ibid.*, p. 585.
5. *Ibid.*
6. *Ibid.*
7. *Ibid.*, p. 589.
8. Sherlekar, S.A. and Sherlekar, V.S., *Principles of Business Management*, Himalaya Publishing House, New Delhi, 1996, pp. 445-447.
9. Vohra, S.C., "MIS Computer", *Integrated Management*, New Delhi, Oct.-Dec., 1980, pp. 5-7.
10. Sherman, C. Blymenthal, *MIS: —A Framework for Planning and Development*.

8

Computer Based Information System

Management Information System, a discipline of comparative recent origin owes its development to computer to a great extent. When people in the management field saw the potential of computer for purposes of intelligence save processing and retrieval, they went about exploiting this potential for managerial functions. Thus historically it was computer that led to the development of MIS as a discipline. True, a manual system of data generation and processing existed in the organization much before the advent of computers but MIS as a formal discipline was developed only subsequently.

Moreover, before the widespread use of computers, many organizations simply found it too expensive and time-consuming. But the computer revolution changed this and todays' managers have at their command a wide range of information tools, ranging from super computers that can modal geological surveys used to search for oil deposits to laptop computer that sales agent can carry with them to record orders and check inventory reveals. Even a neighbourhood retailer or a home-based business can use a desktop computer to manage records of sales. Billing and inventory and with the right software produce newsletters and advertising materials. In fact, the computer may be even more important to these small firms, since they cannot afford to pay the salaries of the people needed to perform such tasks manually.[1]

Some experts estimate that more than 50 per cent of managers already use computers daily—a trend that is expected to continue in to this millennium, when even routine office jobs will be fully computerized. Thus, current and future manageable need to become affective at and comfortable with it.

The use of management information system has grown tremendously following the accelerated growth in computers and their capabilities to processes store and retrieve useful information required for management decisions. The wide spread adoption of MIS began in early 1960's and it has now developed into a major discipline and science. Most large corporation have special MIS groups whose function is to design, implement and maintain relevant management information. Prior to the birth of MIS. Electronic data processing (EDP) was the most frequently used term for computer applications to business procedures and functions.

The development in computer technology enabled storage of large amount of information, which could be readily accessible from central and remote locations through the use existing telephone network. The rapid progress in computer technology permitted the use of computers for comprehensive planning, decision-making, implementation and control functions of management in medium and large companies.

Computer Based Information System—A Conceptual Approach

As Steiner[2] has stated that, "Information flow is as important to the life and health of business as the flow of blood to the life and health of an individual".

Elam and Leidner[3] defined computer based information system as an executive system designed to provide senior managers access to information relevant to their management activities.

T.L. Whisler[4] is of the view that computer is the engine that drives the information technology.

James J.O'Brein[5] has stated that an MIS design should be computerized oriented since this is inevitable for a true MIS. Further, he said that the development design and operation of MIS requires a computer. Robert G. Murdrick and Jeol, E. Ross[6] says that computer is the fundamental information processor and the essential element of management information system.

Despite the fact that the computer is nothing more than a tool for processing data or making computation, many managers view it as the central element in an information system. This attitude tends to over rate and distorts the role of the computer. The vital element in an information system is the human one; it is the managerial talent that designs and operates the system.

One can conceptually discusses MIS without computers, but it is the power of the computer, which makes MIS possible. The question is not whether a computer shall be used in MIS, but the extent to which various processes should be computerized. The idea of a computer based information/decision system does not mean complete automation. The man/machine system concept implies that some tasks are best performed by man, while others are best done by machine. For many problems the man and machine form a combined system with results being obtained through a set of dialogues and interactions between the computer and a human processor.

MIS is used essentially to say for computer-based information. An MIS is an organized method of providing past, present and projected information system relating to internal operations and external intelligence. It suggests the plans cut all the operation function in an organization by furnishing uniform importance in the proper time frame to assists the decision-making.

According to Gordon B. Davis[7] MIS computer-based, means the designers must have a good knowledge of computers and their use information processing. The man/machine concept means the designer of MIS should understand human capabilities as information processor and human behaviour in decision-making.

Features of Computer-Based Information System

The specific features of a computer-based information systems are as following:

1. Organizing and updating of huge mass of raw data.
2. Ability to process data into information with high accuracy and speed.
3. Large computer memory facilitates the storage of large volume of data and information which can be retrieved easily as and when required.
4. Input data can be processed into number of different outputs and for a variety of purposes.
5. Expanded scope of using the information system.
6. Widened scope of analysis.
7. Integration of different information sub-systems working in an organization.

Reasons for Using Computer Based Information System

There is an increasing trend for using computer based information systems (CBIS) because of the following reasons:

1. The complexity of present organizations in terms of size of organization structures, geographically, dispersed

locations, technology employed requires increasingly diverse information.

2. Facilitates the management to communicate the information from top to bottom according to management hierarchy.
3. Greater levels of precision and accuracy required in monitoring production processes in hi-tech areas such as computer-integrated manufacturing.
4. Automate operations, both in the factory and in the office, and simplify management control.
5. Support decision making and planning at all levels.

Computer Systems are Particularly Useful and Cost Effective:[8]

1. When there is a large volume of routine data to be processed?
2. When tasks and activities are repetitive?
3. When it is necessary to store and have quick access to a large volume of data and information?
4. When speedy processing and up-to-the minute business records are essential?
5. When there is a need to perform complex computation?

Design of Computer-Based MIS Model

Establishment of a computer-based MIS is a specialist's job.[9] It involves participation of experts in various skills.[10] The MIS requirement differ from organization to organization depending upon whether an organization is a service enterprise, a process industry, a manufacturing company, a textile business, or a chemical concern. The special requirements of each enterprise have to be studied and analysed by managers and analysis of information systems who have reliable background and sound experience to understand the problem in all their ramification. Thus, there is a need to appoint a task force to handle this.

Many articles and books have described the systematic steps that should be followed in designing and implementing an MIS.[11] Robert G. Murdick reviewed a number of these sources and adopted them to form his own model of how an MIS should be developed.[12]

Four Stages of Murdicks Model

For the sake of simplicity Murdicks' Model can be broken down into four stages:

1. *Preliminary Survey Stage*: the task force will carry out a detailed investigation of the organizational needs for information in repect of various facets of its business. Beside, it will look into the following aspects:

   (i) Asssessment of the organization's goals and objectives.

   (ii) Assessment of the organization's capacity, capabilities and strategic goals.

   (iii) Assessment of the organization's strengths and weaknesses in various sectors of its activities.

   (iv) Assessment of the organization's dependence on external factors and identification of such factors.

   (v) Assessment of the contribution as well as constraints of external factors to the accomplishment of organization goal.

   (vi) Periodicity of requirement of data and information at various managerial levels as well as others.

   (vii) Identification of key result areas and information to such areas.

(viii) Identification of advantages accruing from the computerized MIS as a cost effective device.

(ix) Determination of information, operational and functional objectives.

2. *Conceptualization of Design Stage*: The conceptualization of design involves the following steps:[13]

(i) Analysis of the current MIS as to what worth it is.

(ii) Development of alternatiave MIS design with specific performance requirements.

(iii) Identification of its strength and weaknesses and how to eliminate the latter.

(iv) Through scrutiny of the alternative MIS design against organization goals, objectives, need, capabilities, etc.

(v) Tentative selection of project plan for test, check and discussion with the operational managers and other in the first instance.

(vi) Clearance to be obtained from top management for the introduction of the proposed MIS.

3. *Detailed Design Stage*: Once the conceptual design is finalized performance specifications of the New MIS can be established. This will include the following:[14]

(i) Designing of components of the programmes.

(ii) Designing of the programmes.

(iii) Designing of flow charts.

(iv) Designing of databases.

The task force will thus create a model for test, review and further refinement. After the task force is satisfied the model would work up to the intended level of performance meet the organizational needs it will launch the implementation programme.

4. *Final Implementation Stage*: The task force will now take action on the following finalized MIS design for the implementation:

   (i) Logistics of space recruitment and its allocation.

   (ii) Additional equipment needed.

   (iii) Designing and testing of software for the proposed MIS.

   (iv) Designing of forms for making a use of the system.

   (v) Linkage of data bases with the system.

After a series of final checks and tests the MIS is ready for implementation. Last but not least, it should be emphasized that creation of an MIS design is a long-term task that requires the skills of a variety of specialists.

Guidelines for Effective MIS Design

There are six guidelines for effective MIS design:[15]

(1) Make users part of the design team, (2) carefully consider the cost of the system, (3) consider alternatives to in house software development, (4) favour relevance and selectivity of information over sheer quantity, (5) pretest the system before installation, and (6) train the operators and users of the system carefully.

1. Include Users on the Design Team

It goes without saying the users of the system must be actively involved in designing the MIS. They are the people who have to make use of the system and they know the problems in deeper dimensions than others so far as the utility and format are concerned. They know the needs of information for decision-making better than outside experts. The experts will therefore do well to develop close rapport with the operational managers to understand all the relevant factors involved to make the system really effective for the purpose of decision-making. Management scientist and systems experts have ideas about the technicalities of the problems of the system but what information, in what form and at which interval would be needed by a particular level of managers can better be decided in close cooperation with the organizational managers.

2. Weigh the Money and Time Cost of the System

To keep MIS on trade and budget the designers must pay attention to the cost effectiveness of the proposed system and this includes:

(a) How will the system be developed?

(b) What will be the schedules of time required for different steps?

(c) What will be the milestones to be reached and when?

(d) What will be the budgeted cost?

If managers justify the design and installation of a new system on cost benefit basis overruns are less likely to occur. It should be noted that the greater portion of MIS operation costs go for the maintenance of existing software.[16]

3. Consider Alternatives to in-House Software Development

The high cost of software development has led management to look outside the organizations when developing and implementing new systems. Some organization may find that their data-processing requirements are very similar to those of other business and that suitable software is available from hardware manufacturers of software suppliers. In recent years the wide acceptance of commercial software by both large and small organizations has brought down costs and increased availability.

4. Favour Relevance and Selectivity of Information Over Sheer Quantity

As we have seen, a manager needs enough information to make an informed decision: more information is not necessarily better, although many managers prefer to have too much rather than too little information.[17] In one study, decision makers who perceived themselves as experiencing information overload had a lower performance level but a higher satisfaction level than decision-makers who perceived information unload.[18] A properly designed MIS does not supply middle-of top-level managers with the routine details of an organization's daily activities.[19] The MIS filters or evaluates information so that only the most relevant information is supplied to the appropriate manager. In addition, the effective MIS codeness information so that what is relevant can be absorbed quickly. The information system should also provide top-level managers with data on critical factors and changes related to organizational effectiveness.[20]

5. Pre-test the System Before Installation

Despite the close cooperation during designing of the system between operational managers and system experts, there may remain certain omissions and gaps undetected. To check the efficiency and completeness of the proposed systems it is essential that it should be thoroughly and extensively checked and tried. Only after the satisfactory trial runs, the system should be implemented.

Approaches to Installation of New MIS:

There are four basic approaches to installing a new MIS that have some bearing on the length and extensiveness of the present stage.[21]

In crash or direct installation, the new system replaces the old one entirely. The switch is effected all at once, and there is total dependence of the new system. In this case, extensive pre-testing should be done, since the organization will not be able to fall back on the old system if the new one fails or has major operational problems.

With parallel installation, the new system is implemented and operated side by side with the old system. This approach allows comparison of outputs between systems so that adjustments can be made before the old system is removed.

Pilot installation, offers the organization the opportunity to test the new MIS in operation as it is used by a small part of the organization—for example, by the sales management of one division—so that problems can be discovered and corrected before total installation.

In phased based installation, the new MIS is implemented segment by segment, allowing for operational testing and problem solution before moving on to the next segment.

6. Provide Adequate Training and Written Documentation for the Operators and Users of the System

A training programme for managers and MIS operators is important for two major reasons. Without training and written instructions for the operation and use of the MIS, the organization will be at a loss when experienced personnel leave. Also operators must understand the information needs of managers at different levels so that they know what they are doing, for whom they are doing it, and why. Perhaps most important managers need to understand how the MIS operates so they can control it, rather than letting it control them.

Even a carefully designed and implemented MIS may not fit the needs of users as closely as desired, either because it is difficult to use or because it does not supply all the information asked for. As each new system is developed, it should be made plain how it will change the organizational structure and task responsibilities and how it will affect the job of each employee. It is very important to ensure that MIS operators do not hold the managers to random which may happen if managers are not trained in Electronic Data Processing (EDP) or MIS techniques. Managers must be made familiar with the details of hardware and the software in use.

Problems in Implementing a Computer Based MIS

G.W. Dickson and John K. Simmons[22] have noted five major factors that determine whether and to what extent the implementation of new MIS will be resisted.

1. Does the MIS Disrupt Established Departmental Boundaries?

The establishment of a new MIS often results in changes in several organizational units. For example, inventory and purchasing departments may be merged to make more efficient use of the MIS such disruptions may be resisted by department members, who may recent having to change the way they do things or the people with whom they work.

2. Does the MIS Disrupt the Informal System?

The formal communication network may be disrupted as a MIS alters communication patterns. If organization members prefer source of the earlier, informal mechanisms for gathering and distributing information, they may resist the more formal channels set up for the new system.

3. Does the MIS Challenge Specific Individual Characteristics?

People with many years of service in the organization have "Learned the ropes" and know how to get things done in the existing system. They may resist change more tenaciously then newer people who have been with the organization for a comparatively short period of time and do not have as large an investment in organizational know-how and relationships.

4. Is the MIS Supported by Organizational Culture?

If top management maintains open communication deals with grievances, and in general, establishes a culture with high trust throughout the organization, there is likely to be less resistance to the installation of a new MIS. However, if the top managers are isolated of aloof from other organization members, or if the organizational culture supports inflexible behaviour, then effective implementation of the MIS is likely to be hindered.

5. Do Employees have a Say that How the Change is Implemented?

As we have seen repeatedly earlier, the manner in which changes are designed and implemented affects the amount of resistance those changes will encounter. In general, when manager and subordinates make change decisions together there is greater likelihood that the changes will be accepted.

Overcoming Implementation Problems

No single approach will overcome all the implementation problems we have identified. Each situation must be separately diagnosed and its own individual "cure" prescribed. However some implementation problems can be mitigate if the MIS design process follows the guidelines we mentioned above. Dickson and Simmons have described a number of factors that they consider important in helping managers overcome implementation problems.

1. User Orientation

Perhaps the most critical step in overcoming implementation problems is to ensure that the MIS is user-oriented in both design and implementation. If the system's output fails to meet the users' needs, users will stick firmly, and logically, to their own systems, thereby reducing the changes that the MIS will eventually become useful to them.

MIS design staff should be rewarded by fulfilling user needs as well as for meeting project deadlines.

2. Participation

Many implementation problems can be overcome (or avoided) if future users are made members of the MIS team. Operating managers in particular should have a major say in the items to be included, the disposition of information and possible job modifications. If the entire design and implementation process is taken over by technologists, serious line staff conflicts may develop.

3. Communication

The aims and characteristics of the system should be clearly defined and communicated to all members of the MIS team as well as to users. What makes this particularly difficult is that the character of an MIS evolves as it is being designed and implemented, so the final nature of the MIS cannot be known with precision at the outset. But unless they have a clear understanding of the system's basic objectives and characteristics, team members and users will have constant differences of opinion and the installed MIS will probably not satisfy the needs of users.

4. Redefinition of Performance Measurements

A new MIS may modify a manager's job to the point where old method of performance evaluation no longer applies. For this reason, an MIS that callss for new evaluation procedures and/or criteria must be accompanied by incentives to encourage both high performance and acceptance of the system. The new methods must also be clearly explained so that managers will know how their accomplishments will be measured and rewarded. The notion that a computer can do many thing that a manager can do.

5. New Challenges

Only faster and perhaps more thoroguhly — has a lot

to do with the insecurity a computer based MIS often arouses in managers. One way to reduce this sense of insecurity is to publicize the challenges made possible by the computer system. A new MIS may liberate middle manages from many boring and routine tasks and may also give them the opportunity to use information provided by the system in more creative and productive ways.

Conclusion

Computer based information system is as important to the life and health of business as the flow of blood to the life and health of an individual. There is an increasing trend for using computer-based information systems (CBIS) because of the complexity of present organizations in terms of size, organization structure, geographically dispersed locations, technology employed etc.

Some experts estimate that more than 50 per cent of managers already use computer daily—a trend that is expected to continue in this millennium, when even routine office jobs will be fully computerized because computer is the fundamental information processor and essential element of a Management Information System.

Computer based MIS means that designers must have a good knowledge of computers and their uses in information processing. The man/machine concept means that the designer of MIS should understand human capabilities as information processors and human behaviour in decision-making.

REFERENCES

1. James, A.F., Stoner and R. Edward Freeman, "Management", Prentice Hall of India Private Ltd., Fifth edition, New Delhi, 1992, p. 668.

2. Steiner, G.A., "Top Management Planning", Toronto, Coller Macmillan, 1969, p. 475.

3. Leidner, D.E., and Elam, J.J., "Executive Information System Their Impact on Executive Decision Making", *Journal of Mid Winter 1993-1994*, Vol. 30, No. 3, pp. 135-39.

4. Vohra, S.C., "MIS Sans Computer" Integrated Management, Oct.-Dec. 1980, p. 5.

5. James, J.O'Brein, "Management Information System-Concept Techniques and Applications", *The Times of India*, New Delhi, 1988.

6. Robert, G. Murdrick and Joel E. Ross, "Information Systems Modern Management", Prentice Hall of India Pvt. Ltd., Third Edition, New Delhi, 1995.

7. Gordon, B. Davis, "MIS: Conceptual Foundation, Structure and Development", Internal Student Edition, First Edition, New Delhi, 1974, p. 5.

8. Robert Behling, "Computer and Information Processing", Boston, Kent Publishing, New York, 1986, pp. 82-83.

9. Puri, G.K., "Principles of Management for All", IIMS Publication, New Delhi, 1996, pp. 323-26.

10. John, C. Cater and Fred, N. Silverman, "Establishing on MIS", *Journal of Systems Management*, 31, No. 1 (January 1980), pp. 15-21; and W.L. Harrison, *Computers and Information: Processing* (St. Paul, West, 1986).

11. Robert, G. Murdick, "MIS Development Procedure", *Journal of Systems Management*, 21, No. 12 (December, 1970), pp. 22-26.

12. *Ibid.*

13. *Op. cit.*, Puri, G.K., "Principles of Management for All", p. 324.

14. *Ibid.*, p. 325.

15. Arnald Barne H., "Preparing Management for MIS", *Journal of Systems Management*, 23, 401, January 1972, pp. 40-43.

16. Michael Patter and Robin Mexcil, "The New Programmer The Next Wave of Computer Innovation in North American Business, *Business Quarterly 48*, No. 4 (Winter 1983), pp. 132-34.

17. Ressel, L. Ackoff, "Management Misinformation System", *Management Science*, December 1967, pp. 147-56.

18. Charle, A. O'Reilly III, "Individuals and Information Overload in Organization: Is More Necessarily Better"? *Academy of Management Journal* 23, No. 4, Dec. 1980, pp. 684-96.

19. John, P. Murray, "Managing Information Systems as a Corporate Resource", Homewood iii, Dow Jones-Irwin, 1984.

20. John F. Rockart, "Chief Executives Define their Own Data Needs", *Harvard Business Review,* 57, No. 2, March-April, 1979, pp. 81-93.

21. Capron and Brain K. Williams, "Computers and Data Processing", 3rd Ed., *Men to Park,* Cal.: Benjamin/Cummings Publishing, 1990, p. 313.

22. Dickson and Simmons, "The Behavioural Side of MIS", pp. 59-71.

Index

❑❑❑